VICTORIOUS

Rob Chifokoyo

VICTORIOUS

*A book about a journey of faith, love, and an ever-present
God who keeps his promise to never leave or forsake us*

ROB CHIFOKOYO

To order additional copies of this book, contact:
Xlibris
1-888-795-4274
www.Xlibris.com
Orders@Xlibris.com
702144

For my Lisa and my Hope

You are both evidence that God spoils me.

CONTENTS

INTRODUCTION

"Mara"

Almost 2 years ago to the day I remember standing next to my pregnant wife. "We have come a long way guys." I told the team that was standing before us. We had just completed our third youth leaders conference in Zimbabwe and we had seen almost 400 young people walk through our doors over the last three days. My wife and I along with a couple of our good friends had started a ministry with virtually nothing only to see it grow to this place in just 3 and a half years. So where would we find ourselves a year from that moment in the Reps Theatre parking lot? It certainly wouldn't be a moderately cold spring evening in Zimbabwe that's for sure. We would find ourselves sitting in a living room in Pennsylvania, with the lights dimly lit. I had just come back from speaking to a group of young college students on a Thursday night in Doylestown, Pennsylvania. I had been preaching for half an hour on rejoicing through suffering, which had been a subject I had now preached on at least 5 times in the last 3 months in various places. A year before then it would have just been me preaching about something I had studied, but this had not been the case for me now. I now knew about difficulties and I now knew about suffering, very intimately.

The drive home from The Bridge with Michael Wortell a young 23 year-old man who was a part of the group was filled with conversation about trusting God and following Him with everything. I must be honest in the back of my mind I was wondering why he insisted to take me home because he wanted to speak to my wife and I together. Why couldn't this wait until tomorrow, when everyone was up and alive, I mean it was 10pm? I went with it anyway as I figured it must be very important. So we got home and I could tell that everyone was in bed as it was quite late and all the lights were switched off. I couldn't hear the voices of the two 7-year-old twins that we lived with or the amazingly generous couple that had taken us into their home for the last 7 months. So we kept our voices down as I went to get my wife to tell her that this young man wanted to speak to us both. As I walked into our room quietly, because I could hear the sound machine, which meant that our little baby Hope was fast asleep. I asked Lisa, "Michael wants to speak to both of us." She looked at me and quickly jumped out of bed and said, "I'm in my pajamas!" I went on to tell her that all that didn't matter but that it was obviously important because why else would Michael ask to talk to us this late at night.

So we made our way to the living area and Lisa and I took a seat on the ottoman across from Michael. At that moment there was a little bit of an awkward silence as we tried to make small talk but Michael quickly broke it up. "I don't know how else to say this so I'm just going to say it. I have been chosen to be your donor." Those words hit my wife and I like a ton of bricks. Very beautiful, sweet smelling, non threatening bricks if there is such a thing. I mean even as I write this I'm struggling to even string a sentence together in English that could describe. With those words Michael had broken what had been months of trial after trial. I couldn't believe that this very painful, heart breaking 8 months was about to come to an end. I couldn't believe that the pipe in my chest might actually be pulled out, that I would be able to hold my daughter every night and not just on non-dialysis nights. That I would be able to do simple things like drink more than a liter of water per day and take a shower or swim. I looked over at my wife and all I could see was a woman releasing all the weight and difficulty of the last 8 months. She was just weeping with her hands over her eyes, not a word coming out of her mouth. Michael sat there with tears rolling down his cheeks as he tried to tell us how he had found out this information. Michael had been there in Harare, Zimbabwe 12 months ago at the very conference we had completed. I started thinking back to that week in Zimbabwe and how I never could have thought that this young man would someday save my life. I didn't even think I was sick at the time and I never ever thought that at that conference God was bringing us closer together for a moment like the one we had just experienced in that room. He told us how he was doing this because Jesus had led him down this path as an act of faith. I still remember him telling me that "Rob I would do this for my father, my mother, my sister... so why wouldn't I do it for my you my brother?" We all got up and we just embraced for a good 5 minutes. What do you say to someone who is giving you an organ? What do you say to someone who is willing to risk his or her life so that you may live and get to see your daughter grow up? I had no words in that moment that could even come close to expressing what I truly felt about what he was doing for me. This moment was one that was now among the top most amazing moments in my life. It was like hearing Lisa say yes to marry me and at the same time felt like hearing her say I'm pregnant. I couldn't place this feeling into a box, but that was the closest emotion I could think of. It was a moment. A life changing moment, that would certainly alter everyones life in that room.

Moments

Our lives seem to be defined by these moments. Moments where if we were to be honest almost seem to have some kind of domino effect into each other and create this weird transition from one part of our lives into the next. Some of the most difficult moments in our lives can be the very moments that propel us into who we were always meant to be. So we, if we're all really honest, we have these moments in life where we feel like everything that could go wrong goes wrong at the same time and we think that God has gone against us. I would like to call these moments "Mara" moments. See in the book of Ruth in the bible Naomi has had the worst chain of events that could possibly happen to any mother. Her husband dies and she has two sons who also die and leave her with their wives Ruth and Orpah. Life has been amazingly difficult for them and times are tough living without any men in their lives especially in the time where this story takes place. We pick up the story where Naomi had decided to return back to Bethlehem, but Naomi is going back with her daughter-in-law Ruth, who adamantly refused to leave her side. Ruth 1 verses 19 to 22 read…

So the two of them went on until they came to Bethlehem. And when they came to Bethlehem, the whole town was stirred because of them. And the women said, "Is this Naomi?" She said to them, "Do not call me Naomi; call me Mara, for the Almighty has dealt very bitterly with me. I went away full, and the LORD has brought me back empty. Why call me Naomi, when the LORD has testified against me and the Almighty has brought calamity upon me?"

So Naomi returned, and Ruth the Moabite her daughter-in-law with her, who returned from the country of Moab. And they came to Bethlehem at the beginning of barley harvest.

Naomi who's name actually means pleasant was in a place of hardship so much so that she would refuse to be called pleasant but rather asked people to start calling her Mara which means bitter. She just couldn't bear being called pleasant when she was going through such a difficult time in her life. There just seemed to be nothing pleasant about her life. We all have been in a place where we feel like Naomi. Where we feel like we went away full and we have been brought back empty. Where we don't feel like the God who called us is still the same God who would sustain us even through the deepest possible pain. If we fast-forward the story hundreds of years later we see that God was always in the picture doing something amazing with Naomi and Ruth's "Mara" moment. Jesus is a direct descendant of Ruth and how amazing is it to think that Naomi is part of the greatest story of mankind. Out of those ashes Ruth marries Boaz and becomes King David's great grandmother and the rest is history as they say. We often feel like our bitter moments are all for nothing but when we look a little closer we are actually being led little by little into the destiny we were always meant to reach. We often find it difficult to get to a place where we can see the wood for the trees when life gets difficult and this leads to us at times missing out on the beauty of the journey to being who God has made us to be. There is not one person reading the words on these pages who doesn't have a desire to know what their purpose is. The reality is that through the pain and bitterness we go through, there we find our true purpose.

This is what you are about to read in this book. I am letting you into the "behind the scenes" of my life and letting you see that even in our deepest pain, Jesus never leaves. That's his promise to us and Jesus keeps his promises. You will also read a story that does not end with physical healing but rather as you may have already gathered, starts with it. When I started writing this book I was sick and in need of a kidney transplant. I needed physical healing but what I found, mattered way more than that, I had found spiritual healing and revitalized faith in the only name I could ever put my trust in. Jesus. This is my journey of how God built faith upon faith upon faith in me to trust him no matter how dark it got. It is a book that doesn't end with me waking up from a surgery at Our Lady Of Lourdes Hospital in New Jersey but rather a book about healing before the healing.

I started writing this book as a letter to my daughter. As a way to share the only thing that I would ever want to share with her if I could only chose one thing. The gospel of Jesus Christ through my eyes. This book still is for my daughter Hope whenever she gets round to reading it but I have also realized that she has to learn to be a good sharer and so I'm inviting anyone else who would love to read this, to read it with her. This is it. This is Victorious.

1

First Things First

*There has never been a man in our history
who led a life of ease whose name is worth remembering.*

— *Theodore Roosevelt*

You hear phrases like, "It was love at first sight," or "First impressions count," thrown out time and time again because that initial meeting between two people can carry a lot of weight. I'm a romantic at heart, and dare I say it in a book that will be with me for the rest of my life, but I pretend to not like *The Notebook* to make myself seem manlier. I love that stuff! So I knew I always wanted a beautiful first moment when I met the woman I was going to marry. I have since come to realize the first meeting has power even when it isn't as romantic or blissful as we may have wanted it to be. It's at times when a relationship has gone in a way that we were not expecting that we have to recall or look back to what drew us there in the first place. Recalling that feeling can often keep us grounded in our friendships, relationships, or business partnerships when things get hazy.

#Awkward

There are not too many people on this planet who know how I met my wife. The truth is, it's not a story that easily rolls out of my mouth because it's not the most *When Harry Met Sally* type of meeting. If ever there was an #awkward moment, the way I met my wife is a very big one. First, in order for you to fully appreciate the story and understand what this meeting was really like, I have to describe us and where we're from.

I'll start with what we look like. I'm five feet eight, with dark brown skin. In other words, I'm black. If you needed more detail for detail's sake, let's just say I look like a young Denzel Washington. Everyone who has seen me is probably cracking up with laughter right now, or if you don't know me, you've probably just turned to the back of the book to see if my picture is there. Anyway, you get the gist of what I look like, right? Cool! My wife, on the other hand, is very pale-skinned and has blonde hair and blue eyes. She's white. We are from a country in Southern Africa called Zimbabwe. It is a very young nation and has a strong history of racial segregation. At the time of our meeting, black people and white people didn't have a lot of interaction socially—at least not as far as I was concerned. This is not a thing that you wouldn't expect in countries where the minority white settlers had oppressed the majority black African population. A "white is better than black" attitude was often passed on to the settlers' descendants, which caused a continuation of very segregated values to be prevalent among that part of the population. This meant that the chance my wife and I would ever interact socially was totally not the norm. Which brings us to the story of that encounter.

One night, I was invited to a party by a friend of mine. What I did not realize at the time was that this was a sit-down sweet sixteen birthday party. It wasn't just any dinner party, it was an all-out three-course meal dress-to-the-nines type of affair. Now, I was technically invited through my friend, but had I known that I was a last-minute addition, and that it wasn't the type of party that you show up to with a plus one, I would never have gone. To add to that already potentially awkward situation, if I had known that I was going to be the only black guy there, then I really wouldn't have gone. Anyway, not knowing all of this beforehand, I found myself at a party that I wasn't really invited to, sitting down at a table with my girlfriend who was too afraid to be seen in a place like this with me, and with a birthday girl who didn't even know who I was. #Awkward!

You know those moments when you play with the food on your plate because you're too afraid to finish it and have to face what the next part of the evening might entail? That is exactly what I was doing. If you've never done the food-playing thing, then it's when you pretend-text when you are early for something and you don't know anyone there. We've all done that, surely? Wait, it got worse! This was the night that wouldn't end. Everyone was staying overnight, and so we were there for the long run. After that night ended, I didn't see the birthday girl, Lisa (whom I'm married to today) for three whole years.

I was that guy. Yes, the guy who was sort-of invited to your sweet sixteenth, and brought his girlfriend too. I look back at that moment and think, *Wow, I married that girl. I married the girl that saw me crash her birthday party and who said maybe five words in total to me that night.* The sheer awkwardness of that first meeting will always be with us, and when we look back now, it makes us laugh. But it also makes us marvel. If God didn't want us to be together, we wouldn't have found each other; and after a first meeting like that, we certainly wouldn't have ended up together. The point I'm making is that we have something we look back to that helps us to tell our story. We all need that, especially in our spiritual lives. We need a moment—a pivotal meeting—to look back to.

Our meeting wasn't all glitzy and glamorous like we so often see in the movies, and let's face it, it's not like that for most people on this planet. This earthly meeting of mine points me to a meeting that I read about in the Bible. It's when Paul meets Jesus on the road to Damascus. Paul had an amazing experience that trumps every testimony you could hear on any given Sunday. Yes, even if you're a charismatic! Paul has a testimony that we wish we had. I mean, who wouldn't want to say, "I was on my way to kill and persecute followers of Jesus, and then bam! He appeared right in front of me, blinded me, and sent someone to pray for my healing. Since that day, I have been going everywhere lifting up his name.' Wow! Who wouldn't want that part of his life? I mean, the rest of the getting jailed, lashed, and shipwrecked stuff we know we don't want, but the encounter with Jesus? Wow! We want that! The question on my mind for the longest time was, do we all in some way get a Paul encounter with Jesus?

Meeting Jesus

I remember going to church at most three or four times when I was growing up. Let's just say I wasn't raised in a Christian home, so we didn't even go on Christmas Day or any other holiday. I say all this bearing in mind that I had been exposed to Christianity more times than I can recall. The fact still remains that Jesus wasn't a central part of anyone's life in the household I grew up in. When I was eleven, I went off to a boarding school where they had a meeting on Thursday nights called SU, which stood for "Scripture Union."

Honestly, I only really went to it because it was an opportunity to interact with the girls after 6:00 p.m. And so I can barely remember a single lesson that was taught during those two years. If I was being totally honest, I would say that I did have a realization that there was a God and that he was powerful enough to make things happen on earth. I mean, my mom, my brother, and I would pray for parking spaces when we would go shopping in a busy part of the city and God would "answer" our prayers. We would also sing about the things that God had done in our assemblies all through our schooling years. So I had heard about God and Jesus, but just not in a way that made me feel like either of them wanted anything to do with me. Jesus was for girls like Heather Bekker and boys like Musandu who had parents that already believed and worshipped this God passionately. My understanding of God was almost of him being a really good doctor. The only thing was, it didn't seem as though he was taking new patients. God was a distant and unreachable figure to me, and I couldn't even start to think of a way to know him.

Little did I know it, but after I started high school, my view of Jesus was about to take a huge turnaround. In high school, I became friends with one of my cricket teammates, who professed to follow Jesus. He was different. He loved people and interacted with those who weren't really from his social class or background. Like I said earlier in the chapter, my country was still divided along racial lines, and this guy was very different from your average white teenager. In our first year of high school, we were friends, but we weren't too close. And much like a typical thirteen-year-old, telling people about Jesus wasn't the first thing that came out of his mouth. But he developed good relationships with most of the cricket team and was always the guy who reached out in a way that made you wonder, *Why is he like that?* It was in our second year of high school when he proposed that I join him one Friday night at his youth group. Now, I turned him down several times, and yet he still continued to ask that I go with him to see how "cool" it was.

This was happening during what was a very difficult time in my life. At that stage, everything was kind of confusing. If you've ever been in a home where there is a separation happening, you've most likely witnessed a lot more leniency and a drastic change in the rules that were in place before. I was now allowed to go wherever I wanted and stay over at my friends' houses like I hadn't been able to before. The freedom was welcome for a teenage boy, of course; but it also exposed me to things that I probably would not have been exposed to if my mom and my dad were still together. I started running to porn to quiet the feelings of rejection, and I began experimenting with drugs and fooling around with girls in a way that was very destructive. I also became a very good liar during that time, because people felt sorry for me based on what was happening at home, and so they believed everything I said. I was so desperate for people to care, and I didn't even realize it.

So when my friend Simon, who had a great deal of compassion for me, invited me again to come to youth group and, as an added bonus, spend the night at his house (which happened to be a two-minute drive from a teenage nightclub I was in), I finally gave it a go, and it became a new pattern. We would go to youth on Friday, wake up on Saturday and go and play a cricket match. We didn't ever end up going to the nightclub after youth, which I know now was just a trick to get me to go to youth in the first place.

I don't remember much about those first Friday nights, except that the band was really good and the girls who loved Jesus were as pretty as the ones who liked to party, just a lot more covered up. The biggest thing that struck me during this season, though, was not on Friday nights; but the next morning, at the breakfast table with Simon's family, I was exposed to a father who loved his children more than anything I had ever experienced. I was shown the love of a mother that I had been missing because my own mother was hurting and trying to heal from the wounds of a difficult marriage. I saw something far beyond happiness—I saw joy for the first time.

Watching Rowan, Sue, Damien, Simon, and Gabe on those mornings spoke Jesus to me more than any sermon I had ever heard. I didn't know that first Saturday morning, but for the next two years, I would surround myself with this family; and although I would not actually accept Jesus as Lord and Savior during that time, I definitely didn't mind being around his people. I guess what I'm getting to is that my introduction to Jesus was so gradual and not a *big bang* or *lightbulb* moment. I found myself living a double life, in the sense that I was able to be one version of Rob at youth group on Fridays, and a different version of Rob who still did all the things pre-youth that Rob did on the other days.

My Road to Damascus

Fast-forward from high school to my twenty-third year, by which point things in my life had truly been shaken up. Much had happened in the last seven years. My brother had, sadly, passed away in a car accident, my mom had tried to get us to live in the United States, and it hadn't worked, and Zimbabwe was going through political and economic turmoil. I was a high school dropout, I had pretty much lived in other peoples' houses for years (?), and had left church for a couple of years and gone back. My life had no direction. I had flirted with the idea of really pursuing God with all my heart a couple of times, but it had all burnt out really quickly. At that point in my life, my big dream was to just get out of Zimbabwe and go live in a foreign country. I wanted to be somewhere where I could make a future for myself. I wanted to get out of a dying economy and live in a place where I could work hard and make lots of money and buy myself more pairs of Nikes than my heart could ever contain.

The only problem with my big dream was that I had been denied an American visa at least four times and a UK visa once. I had no hope of getting out of Africa. Well, no hope until a church trip for youth leaders to California came up. I had an opportunity to go on this trip with the youth leaders and then, as part of my "leave Africa" plan, never come back. Door after door opened, and I found myself in a situation that I had dreamt of. I had a visa, and I was going to America. Everything was paid for, thanks to my then "friend" Lisa's dad. Yes, we were friends again at this stage in our lives, and the awkwardness of the sixteenth birthday party meeting was now way behind us. We were both leaders in one of the most vibrant youth groups in our city, and on some Fridays, we would see the attendance numbers soar above 400 students, which was easily twice as many as in other groups around us.

So in October 2006, I found myself in America for the first time, and I couldn't believe it. Yes, I was a youth leader at a youth conference, and I still wasn't a real follower of Jesus. I sang the songs, and I read the verses and played the part. I was a fringe believer and still wanted to live for myself more than I thought I would ever want to live for Jesus. America was everything I had ever imagined and more. But I had made a deal with my then youth pastor that I would go back home to Zimbabwe after this trip on the condition that what I did after that with my valid visa was all up to me.

So I went back to Zimbabwe after the youth conference and looked for money to get myself back to the U.S. the following April. In order for you to understand what was happening at the time, I will have to describe it in detail. I had two brothers who lived in the U.S. One lived in Virginia Beach with his pregnant wife and their son. My other brother was living in New York and working for a bank. They were both doing something positive with their lives. I was stuck in Zimbabwe, which at the time had the world's fastest-declining economy. There was hardly anything in the stores. The Zimbabwe currency was depreciating almost hourly, and much of the country relied on the black market to keep going. Electricity was scarce, and you could easily walk into most grocery stores and find only toilet paper or soap on the shelves. Wouldn't you want to leave that situation if you could? The answer you are looking for is yes! Chances are, the majority of

Zimbabweans, given the chance to leave during that time, would have done so, and many did. The unemployment rate was (and still is) at 90%, and it didn't look like it would get better anytime soon. Zimbabwe lost 3 million people who immigrated during that time, and for a population of just over 14 million, the loss was devastating.

So when I got out of that dire situation in April 2007 and arrived in the U.S. with a dream in my hand, I had no intention of ever going back to Zimbabwe, unless I had buckets of loot to go back with.

Poughkeepsie

I quickly learned, though, that while America may indeed be the land of opportunity, not every opportunity is a good one. In the few months I had been in the States, I found myself farther away from God than I had ever been. I had become the guy who almost got arrested for having weed in the car and who bailed out his friends from the police station for fighting in the club. I was mixed up in a weird relationship with a woman who was nine years older than I was. To put it simply, I was so far from anything I had ever been I didn't even recognize myself. I was miles away from that boy who would hang out at youth with Simon, or go to youth camps and pray for kids who had given their lives to God. I was no longer ignorant of God's presence, but in spite of that knowledge, I was living as an enemy of God and leaving broken hearts and confusion in my wake. That was about to change.

It was the Fourth of July weekend in 2007. To be more specific, it was Saturday the seventh of July 2007 in Poughkeepsie, New York. I was on my way to a party with a few friends, about to have the time of our lives (possibly). There was something not quite right about the feeling of that night. We stopped at a diner on the way to the party, and I remember the moment like it happened yesterday. I walked into the diner, and I couldn't say a word to the girls I was with. I tried, but I just had nothing to say to any of them. To avoid looking like a party pooper, I got up and left the table and went to the bathroom. As I was washing my hands with warm water and looking at myself in the mirror, I experienced what to this day I still cannot explain. I felt a voice from within me say, *Rob, what are you doing?*

I stopped and looked at my hands, and then looked back up at the mirror. The voice, or presence, was still there: *This is not what I created you to do Rob. I made you to proclaim my name to the lost and to live your life to serve those that are fatherless, brokenhearted, and poor.* I was shocked. My eyes were watery with tears, and I was filled with an inexplicable joy. I spent another two minutes or so in the bathroom, but the voice was gone.

Looking back at that moment, I had so many thoughts before I left that small bathroom. Was I high? Was it me thinking those words and somehow I made myself say them from within? In spite of the doubt, the experience was too strong to rationalize away. As I walked out of the diner bathroom—in Poughkeepsie, New York, of all places—I made a promise, and that promise was this: *Lord, from this point on, I will live my life to honor you and to serve you.*

I went back to the table and the girls whom I had spent the last few days with—who in that time had not said a word about God or Jesus or church—said the very next words to me as soon as I sat down, "Rob, how about we all go to church tomorrow morning?"

My eyes watered as I tried to explain what had just happened in the bathroom. I had the confirmation that it wasn't just me but that it truly was the Holy Spirit speaking to me, rebuking me and reeling me back in! That night I accepted Jesus as my Lord and Savior for real. It was not just a prayer; I accepted the call to be a follower of the Living God.

The following day, as planned, we went to church. We arrived a little late, and the pastor had already started sharing. His sermon that morning was all about how he came to know Jesus when he was getting high in his room. His testimony sounded so much like mine. He was saved, and it didn't happen on a Sunday or on the last night of a youth camp. Wow! It wasn't that I thought the people who get saved in churches or on camps don't necessarily believe; but for me that day, it was another confirmation that my story was credible and true. I guess from that moment, I could rightfully say the rest is history. This was the beginning of many events that would lead me back to Zimbabwe a few months later. A place that I never thought I would go back to—at least not that soon.

He's Got Your Number

I will probably never really know *where* and *when* Jesus started pursuing me. I will never know if it was when I went to church those three or four times as a child, or if it was Simon and his example, or saying the Sinner's Prayer to try and impress a girl, or if it was through the amazing men and women I served under in my youth group days. The Bible tells me that this pursuit happened while God was still forming me in my mother's womb. I know I can only recall a real change happening in me in that diner in Poughkeepsie, but the Bible says in Philippians, "He who began a good work in you will see it to completion in the day of Jesus Christ" (Phil. 1:6).

I may not know where or when the good work started in me, but I am certain of two things: First, the work will be complete one day in Christ. Second, it wasn't me who started the work, but rather, it was Christ Jesus himself. When it started is not as relevant as the fact that it *did* start. Did I fall or mess up or feel unworthy after that meeting in the diner? Yes, I did, many times. But now the difference was that I had a constant understanding that it wasn't up to me anymore. God was leading me all the time, and if I fell, he was there to pick me up and get me going again.

A lady I worked for in a school always used to say to the students, "God's got your number, and one day, he's going to call you."

I guess she was right in a way, because no matter how far I seemed to stray, he always had my number and knew just when to call.

***

I guess if you look at the stories I just told you, the common thread would be that God was always there trying to get my attention, and then one day, I finally listened. Like the prodigal son, I came to my senses in that diner in Poughkeepsie and actually listened to him say, *Come home.* I finally looked at my phone, and this time when the caller was God, I chose to "Slide to answer"

(And I know that just made me lose all my Android readers). I hit the green button and took the call that would change the trajectory of my life.

You may be reading this chapter, and maybe you are a new Christian, or maybe you are simply trying to figure out who this God is. You may have just picked this book up, or someone gave it to you because you're going through something difficult in your life. You're saying, "Rob, God is distant from me, and I don't feel welcome." My answer to you is this: Let me take you back to the beginning of the chapter.

I walked into Lisa's party feeling unwelcome, like I was uninvited. Today, though, when Lisa has a party or any kind of celebration, I am the most welcome person at that event, so much so that nine times out of ten it is probably me who organized the event. I went from being uninvited to being the most welcome. Remember that it was me who felt unwanted, and it may not have actually been how she felt when I got to her party. The same happens in the kingdom of God: we get to look back, and before we know it, we've gone from the person who felt uninvited to the one inviting people and welcoming them. The big difference is that it took me years to get from being uninvited to being the most welcome in Lisa's life; but in God's kingdom, this process can happen in a matter of minutes.

There is a woman in the Bible whom Jesus had a conversation with at a well. Jesus exposed all the junk that was in her past and present, but he didn't leave her feeling condemned. Rather, he freed her, and she instantly became an evangelist to those around her. She went from feeling uninvited to feeling most welcome faster than Usain Bolt can run the 100-meter sprint. It's no different for you today. Jesus has always invited you. When we read our Bible, we realize that the only people who felt excluded were the ones who excluded themselves. Jesus is saying, *Hey, you are most welcome in my Kingdom. Come as you are, and I will take you and lead you on a journey like never before.*

Jesus loves you, and not in the same way people have ever loved you; but he also loves you too much to leave you the same.

Why Remember?

This is no spoiler alert. This book is about suffering and going through trials victoriously, but we have to have our foundation set firmly in God's love for us and his pursuit of us. Like I said at the beginning of this chapter, remembering helps us get back to what we said yes to in the first place, especially when things get rough and hazy. Whenever things get hard for me and I feel like I can't take it anymore, or I feel like I'm not really welcome, I go back to that moment in the diner, and I remember how, when I had no reason to listen to God, when I wanted more than anything to live for this world, I picked up and I said yes to a voice that ignited a ferocious fire in me. I go back to that day, and I am reminded that I don't back down. I press on. I remember that I am not who I say I am and I am not who others say I am, but that I am who the great I Am says I am.

If there is one thing I would have wanted to know when I first started going to youth all those years ago, it would have been the liberating truth that tells me that all God could ever do for me was already done on the cross. I can't add to what he's done to give me salvation, but I can rest in the assurance that he did it all.

2

Jesus in a Diner

But like lightning, that light came and struck me
My life changed, and then suddenly
I met The Lord, and it wasn't even a Sunday.

— Lecrae Moore

One of the most challenging things for us as people is the practice of obedience. I don't know what it is about being told what to do or what not to do that makes us want to rebel. We struggle to follow rules. And if we do follow them, often we are looking to see how far we can go before we get punished. The same goes for many of us in our relationships with God. We are constantly trying to figure out how close we can get to the edge before we get reprimanded, much like a toddler who has just figured out how to switch off the TV. *How many times can I push this button before it really irritates my dad?*

This boundary-pushing approach is one of the unhealthiest ways to conduct yourself in a relationship, because it keeps everyone in the relationship on edge. When it comes to obeying God, the first thing we have to realize is that our obedience is not a favor to him, but rather, it is for our own good. When we fully obey God, we are the biggest recipients of the benefits of that action. I wish

I understood this principle far earlier than I did, because I know that I could have avoided years of living with dark skeletons in my closet. I intentionally put the word *fully* in that previous sentence because as believers, we tend to play a game of *partial* obedience, which is pretty much disobedience covered in righteous frosting. We need to know that when God asks us to do something, it is for our joy, even if we can't see it in the moment.

Jesus describes this in a passage of Scripture in John:

> If you keep my commandments, you will abide in my love, just as I have kept my Father's commandments and abide in his love. These things I have spoken to you, that my joy may be in you, and that your joy may be full. (John 15:10)

Jesus is saying that obeying his commandments leads to experiencing a fullness of joy. If you follow him and obey him, you will find what every person on this planet is looking for—you will find joy! Joy is not to be confused with happiness. That idea has been made more popular by McDonalds, Coca-Cola, and Pharrell Williams. But instead, joy is like an HD version of happiness.

Behind the Scenes

In the last chapter, I spoke about how I had an amazing moment in a diner in Poughkeepsie after a very long journey of not really listening to God and halfheartedly following him. The day after I left the church in New York, I started to do something that I had never done before. I started to pray that God would actually change my heart. I didn't want it to be a fleeting emotional plea but, rather, a prayer out of a real desperation and the shock of looking within and seeing how ugly my heart really was.

As I prayed, God started the rehabilitation process and began to show me what I had done in peoples' lives and how I needed to apologize and repent to those that I had lied to, hurt, and left brokenhearted. This was the first tough step in a series of incredibly difficult steps of obedience that I had to take in order to find true freedom. I had since left Poughkeepsie and had returned to the place I was staying in, in New Hampshire. I woke up a few days later, and I prayed and fasted and somehow found the courage to start calling specific people back home to tell each one of them how I had been living my life over the last few years. I knew the truth would shock my closest friends and the pastors who had walked with me, because I had been so good at pretending between the reality of my life and the image I had portrayed to them and others. The first few phone calls were the ones that I wasn't too afraid of—they were to distant friends. I also picked up the phone and spoke to my pastor, and he prayed with me and encouraged me to find a church wherever I was. Even though those phone calls were filled with tearful apologies, the hardest ones were yet to come.

***

I knew it was the last two phone calls that I had to make that would be the hardest. I was going to be telling the two people I had deceived the most who I really was. I remember making the first of those calls to a friend that I had been stringing along and leading away from Jesus for the last two years. All I could hear was sadness in her voice as I told her how I had lied to her countless times and betrayed her trust without regard for her heart.

I was blown away by her response as I sensed a heart filled with compassion for me. I knew something had happened in her life too, as her response to my confession was filled with so much wisdom. She told me that she wished God would continue the work in my heart and that, hopefully, we could still be friends someday. I am glad to say that I am happily married to this wonderful woman today. God had a redeeming plan for our love to be an example of how you can go from being the bad part of someone's testimony and end up being the best part of the same story. This to me is a living and breathing example of God's grace.

As difficult as that call was, I still had one more call to make. It was to one of my oldest and closest friends. I had been lying to her and stringing her along for a long time. I had deceived her and portrayed myself as someone else to her more than I had to anyone else. But when she answered my call, something amazing happened before I could even say a word to her. Before I could say how sorry I was, she told me that she had something to tell me. She asked how much time I had and then started to read a prayer for me that she had written on the third of July—only three days before I had that encounter with the Holy Spirit in Poughkeepsie.

Bear in mind that I had been deceiving everyone in my life, and that I was thousands of miles away from anyone who knew me well. She had been led by the Spirit to write a twenty-seven-page prayer detailing every single thing that I had been caught up in and every problem that I was struggling with in great detail. She was saying things to me that were so hidden that there was absolutely no way she could have known them unless informed by the Holy Spirit. This was before you could tag people on Facebook, and before we posted our entire lives online for the world to see. She couldn't have possibly known all the things I was caught up in.

The prayer she read wasn't just about the bad stuff, but it was also prophetic in the sense that some of the words in that prayer were who I have now become and what I do with my life today. On top of that prayer, my friend also happened to know the sister of the girl I was going to stay with in Poughkeepsie and had asked her in a message for a favor while I was with her. My friend had contacted the girl in Poughkeepsie a few days before I went there and asked that she take me to church on that Sunday. I was blown away, to say the least.

As I wept, I started to tell her that what she had said in that letter was true. I was a lying, cheating, lustful human being, and I began to confess the things about me that were false. Even though she had written a prayer about all of this, I don't think she was ready yet to hear that those things were actually true. There was a great sadness in her heart as she told me that she would not be able to continue interacting with me. Those words were difficult for me to hear, but I understood that it was the right thing to do. Little did I know, years later, we would eventually become friends again, and God would use her as one of the first people to get my ministry in Zimbabwe off the ground.

There are two reasons why this story is significant. The first is that God had me take a step of painful obedience for my good. He had me call each and every one of those people so that I would experience what genuine freedom felt like for the first time. I experienced the peace of waking up knowing that I wasn't living with those lies hanging over my head. The second reason why this story is significant is that God was always at work behind the scenes. He went so far as to place me on a person's heart long enough for them to pray for me, and to go the extra mile and ask someone she barely knew to take me to church at whatever cost. God was the one who was pursuing me relentlessly, and after that phone call, I couldn't deny how much he loved me and wanted me in his family. If I hadn't obeyed him by making those calls I may never have known how his freedom feels.

My obedience, as hard as it was, actually led me to a place of greater joy even in the midst of the darkness. He used whatever means were available and whoever was willing to reach out to me to make it happen. The overarching theme is not whether it was my obedience to call people with my most shameful, personal stuff, or if it was Sara's obedience to pen a prayer that may or may not have been accurate, or if it was Lisa having the courage to forgive me on the spot and not shut the door on me. The point is, it was out of painful and difficult obedience that I found true, life-giving freedom.

Not Done Yet

After a moment like that, you might think that the hardest part was done with, and that I could hold on to that feeling of peace and freedom, at least for a while. It was not exactly the case in this situation. I started to fast and pray every day like I had never done before. I was so desperate to do whatever I knew how to do to get closer to God. Even though I was brokenhearted and lonely, I was only happy to have all the time in the world to spend with Jesus. I was living in a foreign country with no job, no money, and no friends. I was waiting to move to Virginia to stay with my brother and really get going with this new life. And for the first time, I found myself reading a whole book in a matter of days, and I started to understand the Bible in a way I had not before. Through a friend, I stumbled upon the teachings of a young pastor in Denton, Texas, who was preaching the Word in a way that was so different from how I had heard it until that point. I was growing fast spiritually, and I could almost feel the change happening in me as the days went on. It helped that I had entire days alone with no food, no TV, and only books and Matt Chandler sermons to get me fired up.

After a few days of this routine, I started to get visions as I prayed of African street kids, and it baffled me why these images were coming to my mind. I had lived in Zimbabwe my whole life and had never really stopped to ask even one of those children what their names were. I couldn't even really remember seeing anyone talk about encouraging us to serve the poor at the church I attended back home. Once or twice a year at that church, you would see pictures of poor people, and the church would ask for donations; but the dominant message I heard was that God wanted you to be rich and healthy, and that being poor was a curse caused by sin in your life. So even though I was now seeing images of children in need during those times of prayer, I didn't know what to make of them, or what God actually wanted me to do.

It was one morning as I was praying that I heard in my spirit once again the same voice from the diner: *I want you to go back to Zimbabwe and serve the children I have been showing you.* My initial response was, *What? Back to Zimbabwe?*

Now that was a request I absolutely couldn't find any willingness in myself to go through with. Yes, I had undergone some positive changes, but Zimbabwe was still in a dire and unhopeful situation. In that moment, I absolutely thought about lighting up more scented candles and turning up the volume on my Chris Tomlin music to hear a little more clearly. Surely, God wasn't asking me to give up my American dream before it had even begun?

Sometimes we don't fully understand that whatever God asks us to do leads to greater joy, and so we try to run away from him, or find other "good" things to do well so that he forgets the thing that he asked us to do in the first place. I had already forgotten how freely obeying him a few days ago had led to a peace and a joy that I hadn't ever felt. I thought this request was too great and difficult to follow through on, though. So I started to pray more; but the more I prayed, the louder the voice got. It was almost as if every time I closed my eyes, I would hear a voice say, *Go back to Zimbabwe*, even if I was just giving thanks for my meal.

In my attempts to impress God by obeying him in other ways except the way he was asking me to, I started attending three churches at the same time. Don't judge me. At that stage, I truly wanted to follow Jesus where he was leading me, as long as it was not back to Zimbabwe.

My Crazy American Friend

One evening as I was attending a young adults get-together at one of my three churches, I had an encounter with a person that would forever change my thinking about my home country and that would start me on a path in missions for the rest of my life. I was at a stage when I was so broke that the thought of a fancy cooked dinner for free was the best offer someone could give me. On this particular night, due to what I was wrestling with spiritually, I didn't want anyone to know that I was from Africa. There was going to be lots of new people at this event, and all I wanted to do was to eat and hide in the back.

The night was going as planned, but as I was getting up to go and get my second (or maybe third) helping, a young lady followed me to the serving table and asked me what my name was. I know what you're thinking: it must be the "young Denzel look" that caught her attention (just kidding). We started talking, and as we spoke, I was trying to pull off my best American accent to, hopefully, avoid the topic of where I was from.

As we continued talking at the table, the inevitable happened. "Where are you from?" she asked. I told her that I was from the next city over, but she wasn't buying it. She asked me where I was really from because she could tell I wasn't from that area.

When I grudgingly told her I was from Zimbabwe in Africa, she started beaming. Her face literally lit up as she went on to tell me how she had wanted to be a missionary to Africa since she was a little girl. She even told me that growing up, she only liked playing with the brown dolls because she really wanted to be in Africa. She was the first person I had interacted with at that point who knew exactly where Zimbabwe was and what my country was like without me having to explain. It really got interesting for me as she started to tell me how her heart was burdened for the people of my nation, and specifically the children who have been forgotten in that part of the world. As she said this with tears in her eyes, I was so moved by the compassion in her heart for my people. I had never been that way about those children, and I was from the country. Without even meeting them, a foreigner had more compassion for my own nation than I did.

That night I went back to my room, and I couldn't stop thinking about our conversation. I couldn't stop thinking how someone cared more than I did for something that I should be caring about. I thought about the children in my prayer times, and I'm not sure if it was that night or in the following days, but I remember asking God to give me a heart for those children like he had given my friend at the party. The conversation of that night led me to a place where I could surrender my will and get on my knees and say, "Yes, Lord. Yes, I will gladly follow you to Zimbabwe and let go of this dream, if that is what you want me to do." I came to a realization that week that it is better to be in a bad place and remain in God's will than to be in a comfortable place outside of his will.

Met with Persecution

When you take a huge step of faith, like risking everything to follow God, you assume, perhaps naively, that everyone will be happy for you. Most people who have ever obeyed God, though, know that saying yes to his leading may cause further hardships and opposition from some of the people closest to you in your life. I remember talking to my family about going back to Zimbabwe because I felt it was what God was asking me to do, and they weren't having it. They thought I was inconsiderate, and that I was going back to make myself a burden to them. My family said that I was ungrateful for the opportunity I had been given, and that they had made great sacrifices to get me to the U.S. I knew where they were coming from, because I had just been in the U.S for four months at the time. I didn't need reminders to know that so many people back home would have given anything to be in the situation I was in, out of a struggling Zimbabwe and in a world of opportunity in the States. I didn't need anyone else telling me that home was a very hard place to survive, let alone thrive. I wanted my friends and my family to understand that it was with great difficulty that I was telling them my plan, but it was what God was asking me to do. My older brother must have read his Bible a lot during that time because he showed me scripture upon scripture to justify his opinion that I not go back, but I couldn't be moved from my belief that this was God's calling for me.

The hardest conversation that I had at the time was with my mother. She had moved to the U.S a few months after I had, and she was on her way to Canada to seek asylum. Economically, in Zimbabwe, the situation had worsened so much, and the inflation rate was so high that the money you had in your pocket in the morning would not have the same value by the time the sun went down. Zimbabwe was not a country that you would want your son to go back to either.

In addition to the unstable situation back home, I had only lived with my mom since I was a teenager, so her not being in Zimbabwe meant I didn't really have a home that I recognized to go back to. Unless you had walked in my shoes for the last several months at that time, there were many factors that made this sound like the dumbest decision anyone could make. I remember talking to my mom and telling her that God was telling me to go back. She replied in a not-so-happy tone: "Don't you know that the devil can speak too?"

I remember thinking quietly to myself, *Why would the devil ask me to go back to my homeland and serve poor children with my life?*. But if you know what's good for you, you won't ever talk back to an African mom. And I knew what was good for me. She suggested that I go to Canada with her, as Canada was taking Zimbabweans in at the border no matter what your story was. Some of the comments and arguments being thrown out to me were things like, "Don't people here need Jesus too?" "There are poor people to serve in this part of the world!" And so on. Those arguments and the sentiments of my family all made sense, but staying in the U.S. or going to Canada wasn't what God was asking me to do, or where he would have me be.

I think we would all love to stay in the first ten verses of Jeremiah when we feel called to something, that moment of God giving us a grand and bold mission to go on. But as sweet and as beautiful as it is to quote those verses, if we keep on tracking Jeremiah's life through the story, we see how difficult following God can be.

After doing what God had asked him to do, Jeremiah was beaten, rejected by family, and imprisoned again and again. To top this all off, he preached for fifty years, and no one listened! He was doing what God asked him to do, and yet it didn't all go smoothly. The first ten verses? Sweet. The rest of the story? Very difficult. I spent some time attending a church that taught that if things were going wrong, it meant that God wasn't in the situation, or that you were full of sin. I am not kidding. They allowed people to preach stuff like that. I should have known that there was something really wrong when my wife was told by a pastor as she was leaving the church to enjoy the pigs and the pods, and that she would come running back one day.

As I was growing in God during this season, false teachings about everything going well for you as long as you followed Jesus were teachings I had to unlearn very quickly. This often-repeated falsehood remained one of the greatest tragedies in the church today, especially in Africa.

The very truth that we see in Jeremiah and countless other stories in the Bible is that following Jesus may not make you the most popular kid on the block, and that's okay. In fact, it's more than okay. When we start facing persecution for following Jesus, we are in good company. Jesus doesn't hide the fact that there will be a cost to following Him wholeheartedly. If you read Luke 14:25–33 (NKJV), you will see Jesus break down the cost of following him.

> Now great multitudes went with Him. And He turned and said to them, "If anyone comes to Me and does not hate his father and mother, wife and children, brothers and sisters, yes, and his own life also, he cannot be My disciple. And whoever does not bear his cross and come after Me cannot be My disciple. For which of you, intending to build a tower, does not sit down first and count the cost, whether he has enough to finish it—lest, after he has laid the foundation, and is not able to finish, all who see it begin to mock him, saying, 'This man began to build and was not able to finish'? Or what king, going to make war against another king, does not sit down first and consider whether

he is able with ten thousand to meet him who comes against him with twenty thousand? Or else, while the other is still a great way off, he sends a delegation and asks conditions of peace. So likewise, whoever of you does not forsake all that he has cannot be My disciple.

Convert the Try

For me, it was so important to know that not everyone was going to be skipping head over heels about me going back to Zimbabwe to serve God. As I raised money to board a plane and go back to face people who didn't want to see me again, I knew it was going to be tough. And I knew that I couldn't do it without God leading me. I had some of my old friends find it difficult to get over the fact that I had lied to them for so long, and some even went as far as telling me they didn't want me back. I was ready to leave a dream that I had harbored in my heart since I was twelve years old, and I was ready to get on a plane and follow Jesus into the unknown. All I remember about that time was that I was fearful but confident that God was leading me, and I knew that he had better be on the other side, or I wouldn't make it.

When I got back to Zimbabwe, one of the few people who were still talking to me from my past said something that has stuck with me since that day. He told me that I had to "convert the try"—an expression from rugby. If you don't know anything about rugby, I may have to explain what he meant a bit more. In rugby, when you score a goal or a touchdown, it was called a try. You get a chance to add two more points by kicking a conversion over the posts. Kicking the rugby ball successfully over the posts is called a conversion, hence the term "converting the try." We all know that the object of most sports is to score points, and in this case, scoring a try is usually the harder part, but kicking the conversion over the poles can be just as difficult. My friend was basically telling me that by coming back to Zimbabwe, I had done the difficult bit, but now I had to follow through and stick to what God had asked me to do in full and get the two extra points. I had to convert the try no matter the cost, because I had already followed God to a point of no return.

If we look at what I wrote earlier in the chapter, you will realize that no matter how difficult the thing God asks you to do is, it's always for your good and for your greater joy at the end of the day. Converting the try is not for Him but more for you. Looking back now, I know that God was placing me in a situation in which I could learn to trust him and lean on him with everything, to be in a place where my plan A, plan B, and plan C were all him. He was building my faith for a greater battle, which I would have to fight another day; and he was placing me where I would have to rely on Him so that one day I would be able to confidently proclaim that I trusted him with everything, including my very life, no matter how bad my situation may seem.

3

Love Lost, Love Restored

Love is the way back into Eden. It is the way back to life.

— Francine Rivers

One of the greatest traits we have as humans is the ability to understand multiple feelings and emotions at the same time, and we often underrate this skill. I remember when I was about four years old, my mother and my older brother went off to England because my older brother needed an emergency heart surgery. They came back after spending about a month in the UK and brought back two things that I still remember today. One was Michael Jackson's *Bad* album, and the other a VHS videotape of *The Karate Kid*. I was four years old and could barely understand why M. J. was shouting out, "I'm bad, I'm bad, you know it, you know," let alone understand a single full English sentence in *Karate Kid*.

The thing that struck my brothers and me the most was the story about a boy who learned how to fight and who would, by the end of the movie, finally conquer the bullies in his life. We probably watched *The Karate Kid* twice a day every day over the entire school holiday. We absolutely loved it! But in my lack of understanding, I wanted to fast-forward to the fighting scenes because I couldn't understand the English language. Because I was missing the dialogue and the plot, I couldn't appreciate the entire story for what it really was. Fast-forward about twenty years, I stumbled upon the movie on television, and boy, was I surprised. Watching it again but this time with the full understanding of the language they were speaking made the story much richer. It wasn't about getting back at people who were bullying you, but rather, there was a love story thrown in there and other interesting subplots. "Daniel Son" was no longer only a noise I was making with my mouth, but now I knew what they were saying and why they were saying it. I use this example to point to the fact that we have a very shallow grasp of love if we don't understand the meaning of it. The only way to understand what love is, is for us to know *who* love is. We have always heard that God is love. Well, it's true, He's not only the most loving person you will ever know, but he *is* love!

> Anyone that does not love does not know God, because God is love. (1 John 4:8)

That word, that feeling, that very emotion is as much a part of him as your eyes and nose and mouth are a part of you. We need to know God in order for us to love people in the way that we were always meant to love them. Anything else would be like the four-year-old me trying to explain what *The Karate Kid* is about to someone else without fully getting it myself. They may be able to get the picture, but they might think it's a story of an old man who knows karate and teaches a younger guy how to fight off bullies. That, though, is just skimming the surface of what the movie is really all about. My friend Josh used the example of someone who loves eating chicken wings. We can eat the wing and leave so much meat on the bone. That's what it is like to tell someone something without fully going into what it really means or what it really is. You had chicken, but you didn't really have all the chicken you could have had. You only touched the surface.

Redeeming Love

Before my encounter with God, and before actually deciding to follow him with all my heart, love was something I didn't really have an understanding of. I was like four-year-old Rob all over again, watching a movie in a language I didn't understand. I was trying to piece the puzzle pieces together based on what I saw on TV or through what my friends told me about love. With this approach to love, I inevitably left an ugly trail of broken hearts and dark encounters behind me. Even though I had only really dated two girls at this point, I had opened myself up to so much sexual immorality in my past, and it was the ugliest part of my life at the time. The thought that I had been in a sexual relationship with someone who wasn't going to be my wife made me cringe. As I gained more of an understanding of how deep my actions could have damaged someone's heart and were so against God's ways, the pain deepened.

One of the girls I had fallen in sexual sin with was a fellow leader in the youth group I was attending. While I was away in the U.S., she had found Jesus in a very real way and was starting to heal from the hurts that not only I, but every other guy she had been romantically involved with, had caused in her life. I had strung her along and had lured her into my world masquerading as a good Christian guy, only to take away something precious and valuable with one very selfish act. I don't ever want to make excuses for myself, but I didn't really understand the implications of what I was doing when I was doing it. I didn't understand what or who love was, so I passed on my broken and scratched version of it.

When I went back to Zimbabwe and back to the church I had been attending, I knew this would be hanging over my head. I knew I would have to face people who thought of me as that guy who lured fellow leaders into his bed and left them picking up their broken hearts. That thought would keep me up at night because I knew I was a different person, and I knew that they would see it when they saw me. One of the other reasons why I knew I had changed was because before I left the U.S. to go back to Zimbabwe, God began to place this particular girl on my heart. This very girl I had strung along and had helped hit what seemed like rock bottom in church was being placed on my heart. I started writing her letters every night before I went to bed. I knew what she had gone through and how my actions had probably reinforced a terrible view of what men expected from women in relationships, even Christian ones. One letter turned to two, and two turned to three; and before I knew it, I was writing letters praying for her future and about the amazing plans God had for her. The more I wrote, the more I started to see how incredible she was; and when I was about forty letters in, I was on my way to Zimbabwe.

I remember asking her to meet me for coffee so that I could tell her face-to-face about everything that had happened in America. I was hoping she would see the sincerity in my face as I explained. I was truly sorry, and I was truly broken for her and how I had treated her. After meeting her that afternoon, I knew with all my heart that I wanted to marry that girl. I had the "Aha!" moment that we so often see in romantic movies, when the guy finally notices the girl who has been standing there all along. She had also had a heart change while I was away, and she was in love—not with me, but with Jesus. She was dead set on going to college in Azusa, California, and all I could do was think, *Why would God put her on my heart in such a way when she was going back to where I had just come from?* I held my feelings in because I knew there was still healing taking place in her heart, so I went back to where I was staying at my father's house and carried on praying and writing these letters without ever giving one of them to her.

As I continued to write, I began writing prayers in the letters for her to get into the college that she desired, and I started proclaiming my love for her on those pieces of paper. I knew that even if she had to go to college for a hundred years, she was the One, and I would wait forever to marry her. On her twenty-first birthday, when I had written a hundred letters, I knew it was the day I would ask her to be my girlfriend, and I knew that I had every intention of marrying her. I put all the hundred letters in individual envelopes and looked up (thanks to Google) "how to write 'I love you' in a hundred different languages." I found an old shoe box and spray-painted it gold and buried the letters under a blanket of roses. I had a cheap little ring I had bought in my pocket that I was going to give her as a promise ring. So on her birthday, I asked her to come into a room—a room similar to the one where I had stolen something that I was never meant to take from her, only this time the door stayed open and there was a simple shoe box full of romantic words, encouraging prayers, and sincere apologies from my heart. When she opened the box and saw the letters, she wept and wept. I guess we both wept. When I asked her to date me with the intention of someday marrying me, she said yes. The only thing that could have made that moment sweeter would have been Phil Wickham walking in with an acoustic guitar singing, "You're Beautiful." The one thing she asked me was if I knew that she really wanted to go to college, and if I knew that, was I willing to wait for her? I told her I would wait forever to be with her, and that I knew it was God's plan for her. In that moment, God took something that the enemy had distorted and destroyed and began to heal and restore it.

I kept saying in previous chapters that I ended up marrying the girl, and sure enough, four years later, we got married on the day after she graduated from that college in California. I waited, and I have never enjoyed being on a journey with someone more than I do with Lisa. So often we don't hear enough stories of people like Lisa and me. People that have messed up time and time again and don't feel like they are worthy to be in a relationship with God. We buy the lie that Satan whispers in our ears that says, *You're not worthy enough to be in the presence of God. You are too dirty for God because he is holy. Why would he want a broken and wrecked person like you?*

We listen to this lie, which is partly true, because we really aren't good enough for God. But so often, Satan will tell you just a half truth and will leave out the most important bit. Yes, we are not good enough and will never be good enough to be in God's presence by ourselves, but that is why God sent Jesus to die for us. I find now more and more as I speak to people that it is sexual sin in particular that leaves people feeling so unworthy and irredeemable. The scripture passage that freed me from this feeling and from buying into this lie as Satan tried to constantly remind me of my past and how I was worse than everyone else was Romans 3:21–26.

> But now the righteousness of God has been manifested apart from the law, although the Law and the Prophets bear witness to it—the righteousness of God through faith in Jesus Christ for all who believe. For there is no distinction: for all have sinned and fall short of the glory of God, and are justified by his grace as a gift, through the redemption that is in Christ Jesus, whom God put forward as a propitiation by his blood, to be received by faith. This was to show God's righteousness, because in his divine forbearance

he had passed over former sins. It was to show his
righteousness at the present time, so that he might be
just and the justifier of the one who has faith in Jesus.

I love how the Bible shows us that there is no distinction—we
all sin and fall short. When we really believe that, it will change the
way that we look at other people's struggles and how we judge others'
shortcomings. When we hold on to the fact that whether you lie or
covet or sleep around, there is no distinction. We all mess up and
need the same atoning sacrifice to put us in right standing with God.

This truth had the power to trump the lies or the half truth
that the enemy whispered in my ear. When we read this scripture
and take a moment to try and understand what the Bible is saying
here, we are freed from thinking that our right standing with God
is in any way up to us. So when the enemy says you're not good
enough to be in the presence of God, you can say, "Yes, but…"

It is so important for us to know how to say that word *but*. *But*
Jesus died in my place, and I am therefore justified by grace and
grace alone. I had nothing to do with that process. In the scripture
passage we just read, you see that this was a gift to us from God.
We didn't do anything to earn it, and we don't have to do more to
earn it. Though we don't have to work for our salvation, it doesn't
free us to live foolishly. When we understand this gift, we live in
a way that is pleasing to God—not to earn his love, but because
he has loved us first.

Naked and Unashamed

When we dig into scripture we start to see that we serve a
loving God who is capable of redeeming any situation no matter
how lost and far gone it may seem. I wanted to make sure that I
didn't close out this chapter without addressing the fact that God
can, and *if* you are willing, will redeem the things that the devil
has stolen from you. Now my prosperity church background helps
me understand that this line has been used to encourage people to
sow money in the church so that their marriages could be restored,
or that relationships with their children could get better, etc., so I
will tread carefully and explain what I mean.

When things have broken down with people in our lives, the solution to repairing those relationships is not throwing money at God. If we really look honestly at the breakdown of the relationships in our lives, we will see that we have always played a huge part in why the situation is the way it is. The easy way out is to think that throwing an offering in the basket can restore a problem. I know some of you are thinking, *Who does that?* Trust me, these things are taught and do happen in more churches than we would like to believe. But often, the way to restoration is doing the hardest thing we could ever do, even when that means going back and being honest and owning our sin and our part in how the situation became so bad: allowing ourselves to be naked and unashamed.

In other words, being vulnerable before the people we have wronged and starting to walk with God until we have repaired what we damaged. Ever since the fall of man in Genesis, we have been trying to get back to a place where we can be naked and unashamed in front of God and each other. Please don't think that I mean we need to be running around physically naked, but rather, we should be willing to be honest in a very vulnerable way so that people know who we really are and can meet us where we are.

You are never going to be able to allow God to move in a certain area in your life if you are not willing to be honest about where you're really at with him, yourself, and others. No man is an island, and you need people to walk alongside you if you are ever going to conquer the mountains in your life. For my single guys and girls out there, we have to be straight-up honest when it comes to sexual purity. There are no heroes in this department, and we are encouraged to stay clear from any of it. I know in the church we have made it almost impossible to talk about it, due to the amount of judgment attached to this particular struggle. But we have to be bold and find a way to guard ourselves from its repercussions.

If you can allow me to speak to the men for one second: Stop messing around with someone else's future wife and defiling a future mother. You wouldn't want someone to do the same to your mom or sister or daughter. Christian men, stop perpetuating the stereotype that makes you seem like double-minded creatures who can't put a ring on it. Stop stringing girls along without being honest about your intentions, and if you're not sure how you feel, stop breaking hearts by making promises you never intend to keep. These are God's daughters that you are messing with, and having a daughter myself, I can guarantee you that you don't want to mess around with a father's daughter's heart.

Girls, my message to you is this: stop selling yourself short. If a guy is going to date you for an eternity and has every excuse under the sun not to marry you, tell that punk to hit the freeway. For real, you are worth so much more, and I am not the first person to have this thought, and neither will I be the last. Don't buy into the stupidity of getting married for the wrong reasons either. One of the worst reasons for a girl to get married is because of loneliness. I know women that are lonelier in marriage than they ever were single. Don't buy into the lies that are constantly thrown at you through various media platforms. You could end up very lonely in a place you thought you would find eternal company. You are worth so much more than the value we as men tend to sometimes place on you. The only true way to know what you're worth is by understanding the value that God has placed on you. Isaiah 43:4 God says this to his people through the prophet Isaiah:

> Because you are precious in my eyes,
> And honored, and I love you,
> I give men in return for you,
> Peoples in exchange for your life.

You are precious in God's eyes, and he loves you so much that he does hostage negotiations for your life. We also know that he gave his most valued possession for your life, and that is the value he places on you. Why, then, would you settle to be treated like a rag of no value by some punk who doesn't understand the meaning of the word *love* or the value of your life in the hands of God?

He Created the Good Stuff

Another way in which Satan has distorted our view of purity is by taking something that God created and making it look like he owns it. When people think of sex, they don't instantly think about glorifying God but, rather, of an act that goes against God.

Yet this is something God created to be enjoyed in the right setting and the right relationship as something that pleases him. God created sex, and sex is to be enjoyed in marriage by a husband and a wife. With that said, sex is also not a good-enough reason to get married. There is a camp that would argue night and day, especially among young single folk, in the direction of getting married for sex. Even Paul says that if you can't control yourself, then you should get married so that you are not constantly living with the weight and pressure of sexual immorality.

If you really must get married, then do it, but you will quickly find out that marriage is not all sex and cuddles. I put it this way to a young friend of mine the other day as we were driving around town. I told him that getting married to have sex is like moving to Mexico because you love Chipotle. If you don't know what Chipotle is, it's an American Mexican food restaurant chain. Mexico isn't all about quesadillas and burritos, and when you move there thinking that, you are going to get the shock of your life. You will be happy at every meal and miserable the rest of the time you're there. So we need to be able to know what sex was created for, and why, so that we don't find ourselves in Mexico disappointed by the burritos. God created sex, and he created it for your enjoyment. It was not created by Satan so that you can walk around feeling guilty and miserable all day. Even though we may know this in our heads, we need to understand it in our hearts. We need to know that sex is an accompaniment to love and marriage, and that is when it is best enjoyed. When the guilt and condemnation and issues that Satan brings with it outside of that setting have been crushed, it is amazing.

In closing this chapter, I guess I need to take you back to the opening paragraph. I need to take you back to four-year-old Rob trying to watch *The Karate Kid* with very little understanding of what was going on. All I cared for was fast-forwarding to the exciting parts, and I cared nothing for the story that was building up to the action scenes. When we have little understanding of what love is, we just want to fast-forward to the exciting scenes, and we miss the beauty of what is actually happening in the parts that are building up to it. We view sex as an action scene, and we go as quickly as we can to that part and don't care if the whole story even makes any sense.

I messed up big-time before I truly knew God, and I even messed up after I knew him, but the freedom and understanding in this area came as I got closer to him and started to understand his language more. That depth of understanding helped me communicate to others better, not just in words but also in actions. It showed me the value that he had placed on the woman in my life, and even though I know I still don't fully understand it, I am still in the process of learning. My hope is that I don't ever stop desiring to know more about this language.

If you really look carefully at my testimony in this chapter you will see that God is big enough to redeem us and the things we lost because of our actions before we knew him. He is able. Maybe your story is similar to mine, but you are too ashamed to tell people where you really are. Maybe you're smack dab in the middle of an immoral relationship right now, and this is that big-bang moment for you. This may just be God's way of getting your attention and saying that he wants you to live free and not live bound by Satan's lies. Whatever it takes to escape, my advice would be to do it. Stop running away from God, but rather, chase after him with all your baggage and all your chains. They are not too strong for him to break, and they are not too dirty for him to touch. Maybe hearing me out has brought a person to mind that you treated like dirt and left to pick up the pieces. Call that person and do the right thing. Allow them to be set free by your words and see how liberating it will be for you. Let's crush Satan under our feet once and for all in this area!

4

Daring to Serve

But God doesn't call us to be comfortable. He calls us to
trust Him so completely
that we are unafraid to put ourselves in situations where
we will be in trouble
if He doesn't come through.

— Francis Chan

The subject of faith is one that fascinated me way before I was even a Christian. I remember the first time I ever said a prayer as a teenager, I paused and thought to myself, "Do you really believe that there is some invisible being listening to you right now? Do you really think that there is someone somewhere up in the sky going through a billion requests every second and sifting through each and every one of them to see which one He will grant?" And if yes, what was the criteria for the ones God would say yes and no to? I had so many questions then and some of them are questions I still haven't found answers to. Faith is one of the most powerful forces on this planet no matter what you believe. Even if you don't think you believe anything, there is a good chance you probably have faith in something or someone. I have heard it said that even an atheist still has to believe that nothing came from nothing and that's why we are here. There is no escaping the fact that you still have to believe. The fact that the word, believe, is in that sentence implies having faith. So what is faith and why is it so important? I can only really describe it from a Christian perspective because that's what I believe and is the only viewpoint I can use with confidence. The book of Hebrews tells us that faith is "the evidence of things unseen and the substance of things hoped for." Our faith cannot be bought and we understand it as a gift from God to us. My pastor taught in church this morning that faith doesn't come in small or medium sizes but it only comes in large. Our faith is in Jesus, and Jesus only comes in one size. He is larger than life. It leads me to think when Jesus says in Matthew that if you have faith the size of a mustard seed nothing will be impossible for you, He might just be saying even if I present myself in the tiniest of forms I am still bigger than any obstacle you could face. Call it what you may, but I find a lot of hope in knowing that faith in Jesus no matter how small is big enough to make me more than a conqueror over every situation I may ever face.

In 1 Samuel 17:31–36, we are shown something about conquering through faith when we look at David's life and experiences:

> When the words that David spoke were heard, they repeated them before Saul, and he sent for him. And David said to Saul, "Let no man's heart fail because of him. Your servant will go and fight with this Philistine." And Saul said to David, "You are not able to go against this Philistine to fight with him, for you are but a youth, and he has been a man of war from his youth." But David said to Saul, "Your servant used to keep sheep for his father. And when there came a lion, or a bear, and took a lamb from the flock, I went after him and struck him and delivered it out of his mouth. And if he arose against me, I caught him by his beard and struck him and killed him. Your servant has struck down both lions and bears, and this uncircumcised Philistine shall be like one of them, for he has defied the armies of the living God." And David

said, "The Lord who delivered me from the paw of the lion and from the paw of the bear will deliver me from the hand of this Philistine." And Saul said to David, "Go, and the Lord be with you!"

The passage of scripture above is a conversation between Saul and David before David goes to defeat the giant Goliath. David is giving Saul his resume to justify why he should be the one to stand and fight this giant on behalf of his nation. David drew on his past victories and how those victories in smaller battles had essentially prepared him for this moment in front of the giant. His conquering over other difficult circumstances had built his faith and given him confidence to know that God was by his side no matter how great the trial or situation. If you haven't already noticed, this book is pretty much about that: faith building upon faith. And about how when we take steps of faith, God is right there next to us preparing us for the next big thing.

If David as a young boy hadn't gone after the lamb that had been taken by the bears and lions, he might not have seen God's hand protecting him in that situation. If he hadn't had that experience, David may not have had the confidence to go up and face Goliath. When we view the hard and testing situations in our lives as stepping-stones, we walk toward them differently. They become an opportunity to show the world how big and amazing God is. We face those trials with a confidence and a joy that is not easy to explain or describe.

Daring to Serve

After being back home in Zimbabwe for a couple of years, I began going through a season that was very shaky and was taking a toll on my relationship with God. I had left my old church, which had been the only Christian community I had known. Leaving that community meant I lost many friendships. I was working in a place that was going through its own complicated structural and leadership changes. On top of that, my girlfriend lived thousands of miles away from me.

The only real bright thing in my day-to-day life at that stage was the friendship that I had developed with my housemate. I had known him years earlier in high school, but we had recently become reacquainted. I was struggling to find a new church to connect with and was in a dark spot crying out for God to do something. I knew God had a purpose for me being back in Zimbabwe, and I knew that the purpose was more than just grading tests and making sure that kids weren't messing around in a classroom. I had been preaching a lot more at a youth group in the city and also taking morning devotions at the school I was working at, but it still didn't feel like that was all I was meant to be doing.

It was during that time that I had the opportunity to travel to Cape Town to visit friends and take a break away from being at home with the same mundane routine. I had been praying and feeling the urge to do something to bridge the gap between the more affluent church community and the downtrodden in our city, but I didn't know where to start. It was an issue that I would often think of and pray about but had no real conviction or direction to pursue. I wanted to make sure that if I was ever to step out in any ministry, it would be out of an unmistakable understanding that God wanted me to do it and out of a genuine heart for people rather than just a project.

It was in Cape Town, South Africa, where I had an opportunity to go on an unplanned college student camp that I would reach a point of being ready and understanding where God was leading. The camp was in Bloemfontein, a city about 1,000 kilometers north of Cape Town. I wasn't sure if I should go, but the pressure was on when my friend Taf told me that a group of friends had sacrificed their little extra money to pay for me to go with them. I went with a desire to meet with God in whatever way I could because my spiritual life had been dry and I was living off yesteryears' fumes.

At the camp, which was actually at the University of the Free State, I was sharing a room with a young man who was also from Zimbabwe. I didn't really know him, but we had mutual friends. All I knew was that he had a beard and was a very chill-out guy. We went to the meetings and then back to the room and spent many of the nights talking and sharing about what God had done. Those three nights or so with Gwinyayi really shaped what God was about to use us to do in our home city of Harare.

I shared how I felt God wanted me to start something that would reach the lost, the forgotten, and the downtrodden in our city. I told Gwinyayi that if he ever came back home after graduating, he should contact me and join me on this epic journey. I'm not sure if I really knew the implications of what I was saying that day, but it felt like the right thing to say. I didn't know at that stage that Gwinyayi would play an important role in the ministry God was planning.

On the last night of the camp, there was an altar call at the evening service, and the pastor asked the next leaders in Africa to come up to the front for prayer. Those who felt called to be pastors and ministry leaders all went up, and I happened to be one of them. We were led to a back room and were separated as the leaders prayed for us. When they came to pray with me, they asked me what university I went to and what I was studying. I told the leaders that I wasn't in university and that I happened to feel called by God to do this. The people who had come to pray with me gently let me down and stressed that this conference (and calling) was for people in university.

I was so discouraged when I went back to my room that night, thinking that God could only use a person if he or she had a degree, and that it had been too ambitious of me to think that there was anything more for me to do in His kingdom. I went back and talked to Gwinyayi, and he told me that he was supposed to go up and respond to that call; but for some reason, he hadn't. I encouraged him that the moment wasn't gone, and we prayed that night in that little room that God would fulfill whatever he had called us to do. He in turn prayed for me as I told him about my discouragement in going up and feeling rejected by God. Our time of prayer restored a confidence in me to step out and do the things that God was asking me to do without looking for man's stamp of approval to do them.

I left Cape Town and went back to Zimbabwe with a newfound confidence in who I was in Christ, and I was determined to go out and do the things that God had called me to do. I started to feel more and more drawn to lead an outreach into the very dark parts of our community and call it Dare2serve. I planned to start with one outreach to the prostitutes in Harare's red light district, the Avenues.

A friend of mine decided to help get us started with raising money by getting a few flyers out. She actually took the step of faith to come to Zimbabwe for this outreach and serve with us. I had another friend in the area at the time who was also feeling called to join us on this first outreach. At this stage, we had three willing people, and as far as I was concerned, that was good enough to head out and do this mission. We decided to go out on Valentine's Day in 2010 to hand out roses, pray for, and encourage the women on the street. The only problem was that we didn't have any roses or realistically enough people to hand out them out. As you may be thinking, it was also a dangerous part of town to be in that late at night.

I will never forget my friend Phil, my other friend Sara (who had prayed the twenty-seven-page prayer that God used to bring me to faith) and me willing and hoping that the outreach mission would actually happen. There I was, churchless and broke, hoping to start a movement to love the unloved. Two days before we were to go out onto the streets, God opened a door, and a young lady called Carmen got wind of what we were doing and knew someone who could give us roses. She also made an announcement about it in her church (which is now my church). When we arrived in the car park on Sunday, February 14, 2010, instead of the four people we were expecting, we were blown away, as more than twenty people had shown up ready to go out to love, pray, and serve the women on the streets. It felt as though we had an army of God's people armed with enough love to change the whole area and send Satan packing.

That first outreach was a real success, and we were so encouraged by what God had started in our hearts. To this day, I'm not sure I understand why, but there happened to be fewer ladies on the streets that night, and actually dozens of children. The faces of those children who were hungry and dirty and hanging out in the dangerous streets at that time of night broke me. It also reminded me of the images I had seen as I prayed in New Hampshire years before. I finally got it. We were not there for the prostitutes. We were there to minister and pray with those precious little ones.

Dare2serve had started, and we didn't even realize it. In the weeks that followed the Valentine's Day outreach, a group formed that went into that part of town every Sunday. We took sandwiches for the children and played soccer and taught a lesson from the Bible. This wasn't officially Dare2serve but simply a group of people who had heard what we were doing or who had been on that first outreach. Phil and Sara left to go back to their homes in South Africa, but as they left, Gwinyayi graduated from college and returned to Zimbabwe. A young girl that I had taught in high school, Asher, had heard about what we were doing and was excited to join us. That summer, Lisa came back from college and became part of the team. Seeing her passion in serving children in orphanages and showing up for dates covered in sand and smelling like baby pee was inspiring. We were all being drawn to do something in the children's homes around us. That winter, we planned outreaches to orphanages, to old-age homes, and to street corners.

After years of God's gentle leading, and in his timing, Dare2serve was finally born. Over the next few years, Lisa Chifokoyo, Gwinyayi Mabika, Asher Wilsher, and I would lead a group of young and old people into places that the church wasn't willing to go to anymore.

Truth or Dare

God continued to use the principle of faith building upon faith to encourage the Dare2serve team and to inspire us to go on to bigger and more daring things for his glory. We started to see people from all walks of life join our team and partner with us in many ways—one of which was in the hosting of an annual conference. The year before, Gwinyayi and I had gone to a youth conference in the city that we felt was making an impact in the community. The only problem was that it was being advertised to the more affluent and white churches, and we didn't think the organizers were maximizing the impact they could be having.

We contacted the people who were in charge of the conference with some ideas, but they weren't interested in hearing us out. It wasn't unusual for us to get our ideas rejected, because we knew our method of reaching out on a consistent basis to the poorer people in our community was not the most popular approach to ministry.

Churches were still very skeptical of parachurch movements, and activities that encouraged integration were not very popular amongst affluent churches. So we hung back and began to pray for God to soften hearts or to open a door for us to do something.

In early 2011, we contacted the leaders of the conference one more time with a few more suggestions. They informed us that they were not doing the conference again. They had discontinued it, which meant that the kids, who may have been looking forward to that event, had nothing to go to that year. The year before, about 100 teenagers had attended the conference, and we thought that if we could get even half of that number to attend, we could pull it off. In our first year of existence as an official ministry, we were planning to host a conference. We were trying to hold an event that was previously hosted by a youth ministry that had been around for over fifteen years! We stepped out in faith and began to plan our first Dare2serve conference: Truth or Dare.

That August, we saw God move mountains and stretch our faith in ways that we couldn't imagine. We were able to get one of the biggest theater venues in our city at 10 percent of the actual hire cost, and I was reunited with my friend Simon's little brother, who was now a pastor in Cape Town. He joined us with a team of ten students for the conference. It was experiencing miracle upon miracle seeing the conference come together. We were only hoping to get 50 kids to come and so we were blown away when we had more than 600 teenagers and young adults join us over the three days.

The conference was such a success that we ended up hosting it for the next two years, and we were hoping to revive it again in 2016. We brought in bands from South Africa and missions teams from as far as the United States in our second and third years. We saw young people experience God in ways that they hadn't thought possible and witnessed people freed from the bondage of sin during these times. Faith had built upon faith, and we were seeing God move mightily through us. My favorite stories from those conferences are about people from all walks of life coming together and praising God. Seeing the president's son kneeling and praying next to an orphan without even knowing it. Giving teenagers a chance to be themselves before God and know that they are accepted just as they are. I had a young man who had spent most of his life in an orphanage come to one of our leaders and say that the conference was the first time in a long time he hadn't felt like an orphan. It brought so much joy to us to hear stories like that. We did everything we could to raise enough money to make the entire conference free and make it possible for everyone from everywhere to come. Our desire became very clear to us as a group, and we were on a mission to follow God with everything we had. We were there to ignite a passion to serve, to commit to loving our community, and to build a Christ-centered generation.

A Man Named Bud

As the ministry of Dare2serve grew, so did the influence and impact we were having in the city. We were starting to make a real difference, but we needed to grow in certain areas. We needed help with some of our structuring and with the way we were going about fundraising for new projects. We were moving from being a group of young guys who raised $10,000 in three weeks to make a conference happen to becoming a fully fledged organization, which was why we needed more guidance. Mission work in Africa is a tricky and controversial topic. Churches are beginning to assess whether or not spending $40,000 on short-term trips with inexperienced teenagers is actually helpful. This approach of missional tourism is being questioned by Christ-centered churches, but there are also questions regarding long-term missionaries.

On one hand, there are missionaries who want to be indefinitely needed by the country or the cause they are serving and so don't try to empower local ministry leaders. All too often, this results in wasted resources and efforts. On the other hand, there are missionaries who are trying to empower local people and churches so that they won't always be needed to make a difference—those were the ones I wanted to talking to.

During this time of seeking advice from people already involved in Zimbabwe's mission work, I had my first negative experience with a missionary who seemed threatened by the rise of local leaders from areas that ministry leaders weren't typically from. I had known this missionary for a while, and to be honest,

I had been amazed that she knew what we were doing yet had not ever reached out to see how she might be able to help.

As time went on, I finally managed to get her to help out with advising me on some of our structure; but throughout our entire meeting, even though I was being given some valuable information, I couldn't help but feel discouraged. I walked away from that meeting with her feeling despondent. She had said to me, "I would never support your ministry because you can't tell me your vision in thirty seconds."

In her mind, Jesus was an American businessman who couldn't make anything work through anyone who didn't have an American mind-set. I couldn't help but feel that her entire life's significance was wrapped up in being the "missionary" whom everyone needed. I walked away thinking that even though we needed to raise support, if it meant I needed to become something I was not just to get funding, I wasn't willing to do it. After all, how could I explain everything I had seen of God's vision in thirty seconds? Could Moses tell you, after Pharaoh let the people go, what the mission was in thirty seconds? Could any of the disciples give a thirty-second gospel story before Christ died? Her attitude struck me as arrogant, and unfortunately, she perpetuated a stereotype that has damaged well-meaning mission work in Africa: the stereotype that only white Westerners have compassion and a desire to help those who are in desperate need of help.

Unfortunately, that was the last time we ever met to talk about Dare2serve. When I look at my country in particular, I believe it's a waste of money to send a long-term missionary to Zimbabwe from the United States. If a person can't speak the language or can't be bothered to learn it, unless they are a skilled professional and are actually there to empower local ministry leaders to lead, it is a wasted effort. Someone somewhere was spending hundreds of dollars for this woman to be in Zimbabwe to tell young up-and-coming ministry leaders like myself to quit so that they could feel significant and drink lattes in coffee shops and work three days a week. Not exactly a great way to advance the gospel! If you can't tell, I'm still a little bit sore about it all.

I was so put off by the experience I had with that missionary that I thought it was going to be impossible to find people to partner with in any sort of productive and progressive way. I thought that, until I met a man named Bud Jackson.

Bud was a Canadian who had grown up in Zimbabwe and had spent some time back in Canada before returning to Zimbabwe to head up a ministry called Anesu Partnership which is now called Kwayedza. The purpose of this ministry was to partner existing local ministries with North American churches. It would connect churches that had resources to ministries who needed those resources in a healthy and meaningful way. The heart of the ministry was to create an organic two-way blessing from Zimbabwe to North America and then back the other way.

When I sat down with this white Canadian man, I knew he was different from the moment he spoke. He immediately started talking to me in my mother tongue. He knew how to speak my language and was willing to engage with me on my level and not force me to engage with him at his. I struggle to connect with the vision of missionaries who claim to be in Africa for the local people but do not try to learn the local languages. With Bud, though, I had immediate respect for him. There was a sincerity in his voice and in the questions he asked about our ministry. I don't know all the details that led up to me meeting him that day; all I know is that meeting with Bud would someday play a role in saving my life.

Everything he said was so different from other interactions I had had with missionaries. His focus was on building up local leaders in the community. He was a breath of fresh air, and he was also what I felt was a gentle rebuke from God. I had almost completely hardened my heart toward North American mission organizations, and here was a North American missionary encouraging me in a time when I needed it. Even though he knew our ministry had many weak areas, he didn't discourage me but, rather, told me to keep going and to ask him whenever there was something I didn't understand or needed help with.

Over the next few months, I talked to Bud a few times about the difficulties we were facing; but over time, we shared more than just a mutual involvement in missions. Bud and his wife, Mandy started to be a place of refreshment and a source of advice as to how to approach relationship building in places where I didn't have an understanding of western culture. During this time, I was engaged and about to get married, and so I started discussing my hopes and fears about that with Bud and Mandy too. They quickly took to me, and I took to them. If I could describe our relationship, I would say that it is as though they are a second set of parents—except this set has a strong relationship with Jesus and can understand taking risks and huge steps of faith to advance the kingdom of God here on earth.

I had traveled to the United States the year before I met Bud to raise money for our ministry, and it hadn't gone well at all. I borrowed the money for my air ticket, and I had only raised enough money to pay the ticket cost back when I returned. The real highlight of that trip was getting to spend a few weeks with my fiancée, Lisa, whom I had surprised with my visit. We got engaged on the last day of her summer break in Zimbabwe earlier that year, and I had only seen her as my fiancée for less than twenty-four hours out of the five and a half months we had been engaged. So seeing her on that trip was a huge blessing, but the support raising had been what we would term today as an *epic fail*.

In January 2012, at a gathering in Zimbabwe, when I told this story to a visiting group from Covenant Church in Doylestown, Pennsylvania, it was a little bit embarrassing, to say the least. I remember sitting in Bud and Mandy's backyard in Harare and meeting the church group and sharing my testimony and a little bit about what our ministry was doing. After sharing that story, Bob Myers, the pastor of Covenant, encouraged me to visit their church if I was ever going to be in the United States again. He cracked a joke that I may even be able to raise more than just my airfare if I did pass through their congregation. When I spoke to Bob that day in the Jacksons' backyard, I sensed a heart for Zimbabwe and for people in general that you don't often see, not even in pastors. I felt a real belief in what God was doing with us as Dare2serve, and that really encouraged me so much. I was going to be going to the United States to get married later that year and had begun to plan to visit this church in a place I had never heard of before.

My meeting with this group of people became the highest-impact ministry partnership I have made in my life, and my friendship with Bob would someday become one of the most significant friendships I have.

Bud and Mandy introduced us to quite a few visiting church groups and all those meetings brought out good results, even if they didn't form a ministry partnership. I met a church group from Clinton, New Jersey, who would also play a vital role in helping our ministry become self-sustainable and more effective. It was a season of very powerful growth, and the work that Bud's ministry, Anesu Partnership, had helped birth was incredible for the local church in Harare.

Unfortunately, the project came under much attack, as it did not follow the mold of the old way of doing missions and was, sadly, discontinued. Bud and Mandy had to leave Zimbabwe with sad hearts, knowing that their work in the country was not done yet. Their departure left behind much sadness among the leaders they had worked closely with, but I'm getting ahead of myself. Back to the raising of support.

Jehovah-Jireh

It had taken much faith to go on that first support-raising trip to the United States in November of 2010, and it had been humbling to come back to Zimbabwe with nothing. I took the experiences from that trip and learned a very hard but important lesson in ministry that I still hold to. The money you need for what God has asked you to do comes not from man but through man. God can, and will, use anyone to give to what he wants to get accomplished. In other words, money for ministry doesn't just come from wealthy churches in America; it comes from God and from his people, wherever they may be. As it so happened, in that first year of Dare2serve, we raised the money we needed to run our ministry from a group of third-graders down the road even though I had gone on an epic support-raising trip weeks before. God was showing us that he was our provider and that we couldn't rely on a certain group of people who we thought were the answer but that we had to rely on him and him alone.

I managed to visit Covenant Church in late April of 2012, a few weeks before heading out to California for my wedding. I spent a week with the church and was blessed to be with the congregation to see what their church was about. The people had a heart for God, and I knew when I said good-bye that it would not be the last time I would see them. To be honest, though, I don't know if I was all there during that trip because I was just a few weeks away from marrying the love of my life and could barely think about much else. Lisa and I were married on May 6, 2012, in front of our family and close friends. I can say it was only by God's grace and supernatural provision that we were able to do that. Our wedding was the first time I had seen my mother since I left the United States almost six years earlier. What an amazing weekend it was! My wife had graduated top of her social work class, and there we were—ready to embark on a life of ministry together in Zimbabwe.

When we arrived back in Harare, we began to see God supernaturally provide for us in ways that blew our minds. At the time, I drove a 1983 Mazda 323. It was rusty and broken and ready to give in on any given drive. It finally gave up on the day after we arrived home on our way to look at a place we were going to try and move into. Can you imagine being in the car with your new bride on your first day back home and spending most of it pouring water into an overheated engine on the side of the road? You must be thinking, how romantic. I was incredibly humbled in that moment, and not in a good way, I tell you.

But in the following days, we saw God move: family and friends gave us a car that was in really good condition, and we were able to buy Lisa a car later that week too. We were also given a house with a tennis court and a swimming pool in a very nice neighborhood rent-free for six months! We were beaming with joy at what God had done for us because there was no way at that time I could afford to even come close to providing any of those things. I was living out Proverbs 18:22:

He who finds a wife finds a good thing and obtains favor from the Lord.

That year, we saw so much growth in our ministry and added an educational project to our outreach missions. We were reaching more than 200 people every week, three times a week. We had another successful youth conference, and we managed to bring in the South African pop band the Arrows to headline a free concert on the last night. We had volunteer teams come from Virginia Beach and Cape Town, and I had been voted one of the 30 outstanding young people in my country by Zimbabwe's biggest online magazine. This was the part in a movie when there are still fifty-five minutes to go and you can tell that means something bad is about to happen that will send the movie spiraling in another direction. We expect that crunch moment when we are watching a scripted movie, but we don't ever think of it in our own lives.

If we're honest, we always hope that things will just keep getting better and better and that we won't ever have to worry about anything. I think we get to a place where we say, "God, I've paid my dues, now just let me cruise through the rest of my life with abundant blessings and no problems." That is not real life, though—at least not for most of us. There is always both good and bad. Becoming a follower of God does not mean life automatically becomes easy.

God is for Us No Matter What

When I think of how Dare2serve started and how we ended up reaching as many people as we have, to this day I can't help but stop and marvel. I can't help but think of how mighty the God we serve is, who has used an uneducated, looked-down-upon teacher's assistant to reach people for his glory. Right in this moment, as you are reading this book, can you believe that a guy who didn't finish high school wrote the words on this page? It's a miracle, I tell you. It has been an amazing experience of grace to actually step out and do the things that God has asked me to do and to see his faithfulness along the way.

As we look at our own journeys, we have to look at the things that happen in this life as lessons leading us to the purpose for which we were created. I have never been anyone's first pick for anything—except Lisa's of course. But in everything else, I had always been overlooked. In primary school, my headmaster spent two years calling me by the wrong name. When I attended the really big church I mentioned before, the pastor didn't know who I was even though I worked in his office. I have always felt that I didn't matter too much to anyone who had influence and was of stature.

When I find myself in those moments of feeling neglected or overlooked, I go back to that night in Bloemfontein, where they said that they only wanted to pray for people in college. I didn't know it that night, but years after that rejection, I would be invited to be one of the key speakers at a youth gathering at the University of the Free State in Bloemfontein. On the very campus grounds where I was told that I wasn't good enough to be used by God because of my lack of education, I would stand in front of 1,400 high school students (twice the size of the camp where I was discouraged), and I would proclaim the love of God.

God has an amazing way of redeeming situations we can't see hope in, and he builds us up by blowing our minds as we step out in faith and obedience. His plans for us are so much bigger than our own.

You have to know that no matter what man says, God has the last say in your life. Man will never see what he sees. You could be a guy like me, who faces rejection after rejection, only to see God show you that you're not a reject but a child of the Most High. As you submit your life to his leading, he will take you on a journey that will absolutely shock you. You have to remember that no matter what happens on that road, he is *for* you, not against you. My struggle to understand this principle even after seeing how gracious and loving he has been to me would make my embracing a situation that I would find myself facing later all the more difficult. The more we are put in a position to have faith, the more God is putting us in a position to please him.

Hebrews 11:6 reads,

And without faith it is impossible to please him, for whoever would draw near to God must believe he exists and that he rewards those who seek him.

God will continue to place you in situations where you have to leap into the unknown and can only rely on him. He will do this not to punish you or to necessarily test you, but so that you are able to please him. When we look at the situations and trials in our lives in that way, we start to see that the greater the leap of faith, the greater the victory when we see God come through for us on the other side. Those victories give us confidence in who our God is and what he is capable of doing. Then we can be like

David standing before Saul, giving his resume and asking to take on the giant.

I have seen the victories that Dare2serve had with the youth conferences give me the confidence to know that God will not leave us when we take on something greater. I have seen the victories God gave me in my relationships with other ministry leaders give me the confidence to continue pursuing more integral ones. God has used my stepping out in faith and going back to raise support in a place I had failed to crush a lie that the devil had placed on me that I will never be remembered by anyone of stature and importance.

I may not know G4 pilots on a first-name basis like Drake, but I do know pilots, presidents of hospitals, and CEOs of million-dollar companies. So what if my junior school headmaster didn't remember my name? God does, and so will many other pretty important people. God is so much for you that he won't leave you walking through this life with the baggage that the enemy drops on you, but he will liberate you as you take the steps to follow him wherever he leads.

5

Valley of the Shadow

*The idea that there is nothing in the human experience
that God himself
has not suffered, even losing a child, is sustaining.
And the idea that in His resurrection, Jesus' scars
became His glory is empowering.*

—Tim Keller

One unchanging truth life has taught me is that bad news doesn't have an ideal timeline for when it will arrive. The brightest, most beautiful of mornings could bring with it the worst news of your life. I remember one such Saturday morning when I was fifteen. In the midst of the sunshine and blue sky, I got some of the worst news I would ever get. I woke up that morning, and everything was normal; yet when I look back now, nothing about it was normal at all. When I remember that day, it almost seems as though everything moved in slow motion.

My mom got up early to go and get her hair done, and my dad had also gone off to run some errands. (If you have been following my story attentively, you will recall that my parents had separated when I was thirteen, but at this point, my mom had moved back in with my dad to try to patch things up and give their marriage a second chance.) One of my older brothers had also left the house early that day to go to a track meet out of town. This left our maid (it is very common to have a live in house keeper in a Zimbabwean household) and me alone at home. It was about 9:00 a.m. when I heard a loud knock at the gate and asked if she could go and see who it was.

I remember looking through the window and seeing a police car and a policeman talking to her, and I instinctively knew that whatever the situation was, it wasn't good. For some reason I still can't explain, I ran as far from the house as I could. Maybe I knew that whatever the police were there for, I wasn't ready to hear it. As I tried to muster up the courage to go back into the house, I saw her walk toward me, weeping before I could get back to the house. She stopped, and through her crying and whimpering, she uttered the worst news I had ever heard: "Patrick is dead."

It was a bright blue autumn morning, the birds were singing in the trees, the sun was bright in the sky. It was not the kind of day that was fitting to hear that your brother had died in a car accident. The week before, we had seen my other brother, Takunda (T.J), get through a very difficult set of examinations, called O levels, with flying colors. It was a really good week for my family right up until that moment on that morning.

Even as I write this, it is difficult to go back to that day. If you have ever suddenly lost someone that you love, you will know what I mean. I'm fairly certain I had woken up happy that morning, and even though I don't remember all the details of that day, I'm sure everything had been pretty normal for a Saturday morning. A few hours later, my parents came back home. My dad couldn't tell my mom the news while he was driving, so he had waited until they were at home. I saw them walk in to the house, and she looked at my little brother and me, and knew something was wrong.

My dad shut the bedroom door behind him, and after a few seconds of silence, I heard a cry that my ears had never heard before. For the rest of that day, all I heard was crying and wailing as more and more people arrived at our house to comfort my family. Any happiness that we had in us or had experienced before 9:00 a.m. that Saturday had been snatched away with just one sentence, one instant, one moment. It was gone. Patrick was gone forever. We would never see his smile, hear his jokes, or touch his face again.

Happiness is such a cheap version of joy. It can be here one moment and be gone the very next. The Bible is constantly pointing us to joy rather than happiness, because joy is not dictated by the same elements that happiness is. We can be joyful through trials; we may not necessarily always be happy, but we can always have joy. And more than that, when we have the joy of the Lord, we are told that this joy will be our strength. When we have this joy, it doesn't matter what we have to go through. It will strengthen us to face another day and keep going.

Sunshine before the Rain

Lisa and I had been married for only five months. We were living in a blessing of a house and seeing our ministry grow from strength to strength. I had been supporting us and most of our ministry projects by working part-time in a school, and then working for Dare2serve in the afternoon. The ministry was growing fast, but things were beginning to fall through the cracks because there wasn't anyone focusing on it full-time.

One morning, as I was praying, I once again heard that voice tell me that I needed to quit my job and go into the ministry full-time. You can imagine my initial response to that: *You must be kidding me!* I had been married for just five months, and I was supposed to quit a job that provided income not only for my family but for helping the ministry go forward? I had thought the experience in Poughkeepsie was a stretch of my sanity, but this request was even more ridiculous. How would we survive? You need money to buy food, and you need food to live, right?

God knew all the answers to my questions, though; and the more I prayed, the more he gave me a peace that it really was him talking to me. I finally decided that I would go through with it—as long as Lisa was in agreement with me. A part of me said that knowing that my sensible wife was probably going to be shocked and wouldn't be on board with the idea because it would put us in a very difficult position so early in our marriage. We had been given six months rent-free in this house, and it was month number 5—meaning we would have to move out and start paying rent soon.

So quitting my job and losing our primary source of income didn't make any sense. I was sure she would feel the same way I did. So as I sat down to tell Lisa what I was feeling in my heart, trust me, I didn't make the step of faith look enticing at all. I asked what she thought and her response shocked the socks off me. Lisa told me that she had a feeling of peace about the decision to leave my job, and if God wanted us to go without for the sake of the gospel, she was in. I was blown away by her faith, but now I was also more afraid than I had been before asking her. The statement was actually out of my mouth, and I probably had to follow through with it now.

There was, however, still the hurdle of quitting my job in order to take this step of faith. Leaving my job was one very real hurdle that I wasn't in a hurry to jump. I thought my boss really wouldn't want me to leave; and surely, God wouldn't want me to dishonor my word by leaving her short-staffed. Lisa had been full of faith, and that was great; but thankfully, my boss would be the stopping point in this crazy plan, and I could still appear to have been as obedient as I could be. With this in mind, I went to speak to my boss the following week about what God was asking me to do. Her response also shocked me as she told me that she had been watching me for the last few weeks and wondering when I would come and tell her that I needed to go into full-time ministry.

After that moment, I had no more excuses. I knew that God wanted me to obey him, and I knew I had to trust him. I had seen him move and do powerful things before. I had to trust him and hope that once again, he would be on the other side of this big decision.

Two days after I had told my boss I was going to trust God and do what he was asking me to do, I received an e-mail from the owner of the house we were staying in asking us if we would like to stay for another six months rent-free!

What an amazing God we serve. It's almost as though I had to take the step of faith and quit my job before he would reveal that he had already taken care of our needs.

Not Even a Pizza

We lived on what seemed like manna from heaven in the following months. Going full-time helped us further our ministry, get an office, and have our first interns work with us; but life was financially tumultuous. Even though we had a roof over our heads, we didn't ever seem to have any money left over for anything apart from what was really needed. The reason I say it was like manna is because if someone blessed us with $100 on a Sunday, our car would die on the Monday, and it would cost $100 to fix. We couldn't ever store it up. Things like this would happen all the time. Out of frustration, I would always think, *God, why not just give us $110 so that we could have $10 left over for a pizza?*

After months and months of this financial pressure, I decided to try and raise support in the United States one more time. I thought that maybe if we planned our trip properly this time and we met with churches where we actually had relationships, we would be able to raise the money to have a fulltime staff member and get some of our projects functioning more effectively. The dilemma with going back to the States was that it would cost $3,500 for my wife and me to go. If we were to fund-raise any less than that, it wouldn't be worth it.

Another dilemma was how we would get the money to go there anyway. I mean, when $10 is hard to come by, $3,500 is a lot of money.

God quickly provided the solution to one of those questions when I received a call from a friend in Hong Kong saying that he wanted to pay for my ticket, so that covered me but left Lisa still needing a ticket. We sent out letters to people we knew, letting them know what we were planning; and we checked our bank account for a miracle every day. The logistical flaw in our plan was that you couldn't deposit money into our bank account from the United States, and we had only asked our friends from there to help us.

In spite of this, one evening, knowing we needed exactly $1,400 for Lisa to be able to go, we checked our bank account, which had only $90 in it earlier that morning to find the balance was miraculously at $1,490! We frantically tried to find out who had deposited the money, but the bank wouldn't let us access the information. I guess it was God's way of reminding us that it was he who had provided, and that who he had used to help didn't really matter at the time. We found out a few days later that it had been a family member who had sacrificially given us the money in the midst of going through their own financial hard times. The support for our vision meant so much to us. So it was official: we were going to America for six weeks to raise enough money to have a full-time staff member for the first time in Dare2serve's existence.

God's thoughts are not our thoughts. He is infinitely wiser and more intelligent than even the smartest person among us, but I think there are moments where he takes something simple and silly to help us understand his truth. We had visited five out of the six churches we had planned to see, and had been in the United States for almost five weeks, and had only managed to raise a couple of hundred dollars. We had already used this money for meals and tickets, and we only had one week and one church left to see.

Once again, the fundraising trip had not gone as planned, and Lisa and I were losing hope. At this point, we were staying in New Jersey, and I clearly remember a time of praying in the backyard. I was shaking my fist at heaven and thinking, *Wow Lord, why did you bring us all this way just to let us down?* I felt the same way Jeremiah had felt in the Bible when he cried out to God in frustration because following God had made his life incredibly difficult. That afternoon in the backyard, I cried out to God in honesty of my disappointment in feeling like he led me down the wrong path. After I was finished with being silly and venting my misplaced frustration at the Creator of the universe, I was hit with a sense of peace. The peace that surpasses my general understanding and the peace that left me saying, "Your will, Lord, no matter what. Your will."

After this pivotal time of prayer, we went on to our last church, which happened to be Covenant Church in Doylestown with Pastor Bob Myers whom I had met back in Zimbabwe a few years earlier. I had visited the church the year before on my way to getting married in California, and I had connected well with a few people in the congregation. We were staying with a family that had felt called to take care of visiting missionaries, and our arrival had been very pleasant. I had shared our step of faith with one of the ladies on the missions team at the church earlier the year before when I quit my job, and I knew she was praying for us; but I wasn't ready for what was about to happen.

On our second day there, we were told that there was an "epic luncheon" being prepared for us. We arrived at the house for the luncheon, and it was amazing. There was a chef making the food and the house itself looked like something out of *Downton Abbey*. It had ten bathrooms, for crying out loud! After we had eaten our meal, which I thought was the whole point of the afternoon, the team sat Lisa and me down. There were about thirteen people in total, and they each shared with us why they were there that afternoon. They called themselves the Mustard Seed Group, and they were all from different churches in the Doylestown area, who had heard of our step of faith through a lady at Covenant Church. God moved the group to do a fundraising night for us by selling all their secondhand bags and hats, and even melting down some of their jewelry and selling it. They had no idea how much money they would raise, and were so blown away by what God had done through them that night.

As we sat there that afternoon in a beautiful house, they handed my wife a check, and as she looked down at it, she started to weep. Now, Lisa is a crier, and so I knew it was difficult to gauge the amount of the check by her response. As she was crying, some of the tears landed pretty close to that valuable piece of paper, so I quickly looked at her and said, "Please, not on the check, honey. We need it!"

She eventually handed it to me, and on that piece of paper was enough money to support a full-time staff member for the next seven months. We had been given $4,700, and what was funny was that the group had held their fundraising night three months before we even got to the United States. So when I was crying out in that backyard in New Jersey—"Lord, why have you forsaken us?"—he had already taken care of it months before. God had pulled an Adam on me and had taken care of my greatest need while I was sleeping.

As if this wasn't enough, there was one more thing that happened to really let me know that God was in full control of our lives and ministry. The people from the Mustard Seed Group handed my wife a bag with some of the things they had kept for her from the sale night. There was a nice handbag and some earrings. Now, I had been sharing the story of "manna from heaven" everywhere we had been for the last five weeks, but I had not uttered a word of that story to this group. (Remember how God would provide for us but wouldn't even give us a little extra for a pizza?)

Well, after giving Lisa her gifts, the ladies at the luncheon looked at me and told me that there was only girly stuff at the sale, so there was nothing for me except the thing God had told them to give me. I reached into the bag, and as I looked at the piece of paper in my hand, I was brought to tears. It was a coupon for a Domino's large pizza! God has such an amazing sense of humor! He was saying, *Rob, I will take care of you, and if a pizza is what you want, I've got you!*

I sat there thinking, *A pizza?* I should have aimed higher than a pizza! I preached at church that Sunday, and God's provision continued to be poured out on us. By the time we left Covenant for Zimbabwe, we had raised a total of $15,000 for our ministry. God had gone above and beyond our limited expectations, and the generosity of this congregation had left us humbled beyond words. I had not experienced such blessing before, and life couldn't have been better. God had affirmed our steps of obedience and faith.

The Rain

We experienced so much joy and great breakthrough in our lives at that time. After leaving the United States, we arrived home and were given yet another five months in the house rent-free. I was earning an income doing what I was called to do, and we had just discovered that we were pregnant. Dare2serve had hosted another successful youth conference, and in addition to that, Lisa and I were also heading up the youth ministry at our church, which was going well. I was getting invitations to fly to South Africa to preach at huge gatherings, as well as other opportunities in the region to earn money for the ministry. The sun was shining brightly, and God was taking care of us so well. Life was just beautiful! It was on a Friday night at one of our youth meetings when all of this came to a sudden stop. I suddenly felt nauseous as I was speaking and had to run out midsentence to throw up in the bathroom. I had been ill earlier that year after returning from our US trip and had been told that I had high blood pressure. My doctor said that apart from AIDS, the big killer in Zimbabwe was high blood pressure. He prescribed some medication and told me I needed to take the situation seriously, so I did. Unfortunately, I would not really recover from that night.

I now know that the high blood pressure diagnosis I had been given earlier was incorrect, but let me not get ahead of myself. I spent the next ten days in bed and lost weight quickly, as I couldn't really eat or drink anything. I had never been that sick in my life, and I couldn't understand what was going on with me. I went to see the doctor again, and he told me it was just a stomach bug, and that I needed to take antibiotics to get me back on my feet. So I did just that. I trusted my doctor so much that I even traveled to go and be a groomsman at my high school friend Simon's wedding in South Africa. I was young and relatively fit, and so I kept thinking that the nausea would go away and I would wake up feeling better. But it just wasn't happening.

Every night before I went to bed, I would vomit out everything I had eaten. When I returned from the wedding and was still sick, I went back to the doctor, and he told me the same news—it was just a stomach bug, and it needed time. He even drew me a diagram to show me how it was all working in my stomach, and I believed him. "Take the meds, and you'll be better," he said and handed me another prescription. Only this time, the medication made me worse. The nights were especially terrible. I remember one particular night, I woke up to use the bathroom. I was out of energy and in terrible pain, and I fainted. My body was giving up, and I was certain that neither the doctors nor I knew what was really wrong. Everything in my body was changing so quickly. On top of me being sick, the owner of the house we were staying in had suddenly decided to sell the house, so we were given a month's notice to move out.

I was very sick but didn't know what more I could do to get better. I had already seen the doctor twice, and the medication wasn't working. But one night, after I almost choked on my own vomit, Lisa, weeping, asked me to let her take me to the emergency room. She knew that they would draw my blood for testing, and maybe get to the bottom of this illness. I agreed to let her take me the next day. In the morning, we went to the emergency room thinking all I needed was an injection to get rid of the nausea, and then I would be back home to help finish moving into our new place. But I could barely sit up without feeling as though I had just run a marathon. I couldn't figure out what was happening, and I didn't know it at the time, but I was actually dying.

The day we went into that emergency room was bright and sunny, much like the autumn morning my brother Patrick died. The birds were singing, and the sky was blue. Lisa and I joked around as we got ready to go to the hospital. We got there, and the doctor did a few tests and came back after an hour with the results. He walked into the little room, closed the curtain behind him, and started to tell me that I was very sick. The blood tests had come back showing that I had renal failure. I had to be immediately admitted into the high dependency unit, and I needed dialysis to live.

I had no idea at the time what renal failure was, never mind what dialysis meant; but looking at the way Lisa was crying, I knew it was serious. She cried as I rubbed her arm, telling her that it was going to be okay. I was thinking that dialysis was a pill, and I would be back on my feet in no time. Slowly, Lisa explained to me what was going on. She rushed around in the midst of her own tears and panic to call my brother and my dad. The gravity of the situation was sinking in slowly, but to be honest, I was too sick to even worry about the details. I only wanted to get better and back on my feet, whatever that took. A good friend of ours brought me a pillow, and she sat with me holding my hand in my darkest hour. I will never forget the comfort that I felt from her in that cold hospital room.

As is often the case in Zimbabwe, there were no beds in the hospital we were in, so my wife had to drive around town to find a hospital with a bed available in the high dependency unit. That day, I took my first ambulance ride as a patient with wires and tubes coming from all over my body. As I lay in the ward that night, with heart monitors measuring my pulse, blood pressure cuffs beeping, and people who were close to death all around me, all I thought was, *This isn't really happening to me, is it? How is this happening to me?*

That night in hospital, for the first time in a very long time, it felt like God was silent; and even though I was questioning him, there were no answers coming back. Not a clear voice like the one I had heard in Poughkeepsie. Not a challenging word like the one I had heard asking me to go back to Zimbabwe. Not a quiet nudge like the one asking me to quit my job. Nothing but silence. Silence, darkness, and the beeping heart monitors at the St. Anne's HDU Ward. If it wasn't me lying in that bed, I could have recited every appropriately encouraging verse to someone else. But no passage of scripture helped me close my eyes that night. Was this really it? After all I had seen God do in my life, was this really how it would end? As much as I asked that and got a response, it still didn't feel like the end to me. And now I know it was another moment and another opportunity to see how amazing and how powerful this God we serve is. I didn't fully understand it then, but that clear voice would come back. The more I sought God, the more I realized that he was doing something that he had been preparing Lisa and me to go through.

Jesus Is Always on Time

I spent eight days at the hospital and was more and more encouraged each day by the news the doctor brought. I prayed, read the Bible, and quoted verses to my wife and to myself as often as possible. The doctor was optimistic that I could spend Christmas at home, and I was looking forward to that. Even though I knew I wasn't 100 percent back to normal, I was ready to leave the hospital and be at home with my wife. My kidney function had improved slightly but was still below 10 percent. But I remained confident that I had been healed, and that this traumatic experience was all behind us. The doctor released me to go home on Christmas Eve. Lisa didn't think it was a good idea, but I wanted to be out of hospital, so I went with the doctor's opinion. At this stage, the doctors thought that I may not need dialysis after all; and even though my creatinine levels hadn't come down to a place where I should be out of the hospital, they wanted to see if the levels would continue to go down at home without the assistance of IV fluid.

At home, I spent much of Christmas in pain and struggling to breathe. I still thought this was a turn for the better, and that I would slowly get back on my feet. I had two days at home and planned to go for more tests on the weekend to see if my levels had gone up again. I prayed, I tried my best to drink water and not vomit when I ate, but it didn't work. I felt myself getting worse as the days progressed. By the time the weekend came, I knew that the tests would be bad even though I had prayed for a miracle to happen. I failed the tests; my levels were right back to where they were when I was first admitted. I knew I had to go back to the HDU ward and would be starting 2014 from a hospital bed.

The doctor told us that I had to start dialysis as soon as possible. I went back into hospital that day a very defeated person. This time I didn't even want to see a Bible near me, and I didn't want to speak to Jesus anymore. I felt that he had left me and abandoned me in my most desperate time of need. My messed-up view of who I thought God was, was revealed by my actions during that time. I knew better, but at that moment, I was acting as though God existed to make me happy and comfortable. As long as I did everything he asked, he would do whatever I asked him. When you feel like this, you have to go back to the Bible and read about some of the things the people whom Jesus loved had to endure. Those stories can give us perspective and help quiet down the whispers of the enemy in our dark moments. Even though I knew this, my heart was so far from those truths. In my selfish human nature, I just wanted Jesus to take this pain away.

John 11 is a passage of scripture that I have preached on many times, but my heart in this matter really showed me that I didn't understand what I had been preaching about.

> Now a certain man was ill, Lazarus of Bethany, the village of Mary and her sister Martha. It was Mary who anointed the Lord with ointment and wiped his feet with her hair, whose brother Lazarus was ill. So the sisters sent to him, saying, "Lord, he whom you love is ill." But when Jesus heard it he said, "This illness does not lead to death. It is for the glory of God, so that the

Son of God may be glorified through it." Now Jesus loved Martha and her sister and Lazarus. So, when he heard that Lazarus was ill, he stayed two days longer in the place where he was.

When I look at this Bible story and the way I felt at that moment, the things I said didn't make sense to me after reading those first six verses. I was sick, and I was back in hospital, and I saw what was happening in my life and said, "Jesus, you don't care about me."

In the story, Lazarus was ill, and Jesus was close to him and his family; the passage even stresses that he loved them all, yet Lazarus was still going through what was probably the lowest point of his life. Jesus loved Lazarus and he let him suffer? Why would Jesus do that? Why would the Bible say that Jesus loved him yet he left him to die alone? These are all questions the Holy Spirit prompted me to look at while I was on my hospital bed. I was looking at the situations in my life and using them as an indication of how God felt about me.

Without even knowing it, I was basing God's goodness on how comfortable I felt and how good my life was at that very moment. I knew better than to actually say that out loud, because we all know that is bad theology, right? But knowing that didn't stop me from thinking it. For a very dark moment, I believed it too. What about the silence I was experiencing? What about the delay in coming to my rescue with healing? But it was the same for Lazarus. In verse 6, it says Jesus heard that Lazarus was ill and that he stayed two whole days longer where he was. He didn't stop everything at the drop of a hat to run to Lazarus's rescue to take care of his illness. He stayed two days after hearing the news, which meant Lazarus probably wouldn't make it. As we read further, we will see that by the time Jesus arrived, Lazarus had already been dead four days (John 11:17). How many times have we asked that same question of Jesus that Martha asks in verse 21—"If you had just been here earlier, Jesus, it wouldn't be this bad."

I can think of two reasons that Jesus may have delayed his return. The first reason may have been the fact that even before Lazarus had a fever, Jesus knew that he was going to be sick. This illness didn't take Jesus by surprise in the same way that it had taken Mary, Martha, and Lazarus himself by surprise. Jesus was calm because there was nothing the ladies were telling him that he didn't already know. My second reason is that Jesus already knew why Lazarus was sick, and he already knew what the outcome was going to be. He actually gave Mary and Martha the assurance that Lazarus would not die because what was about to happen was for the glory of God, to be made known to people who didn't know him (John 11:4).

When I was reminded about this scripture in my hospital bed, I was struck with the truth that God knew all along that I had only one kidney. He knew all along that when I turned thirty, that one kidney was going to fail. The only person between God and me who was getting this news as a surprise was me. He hadn't been taken by surprise; neither had he left me alone, nor was he being silent. Rather, just as when he told the Mustard Seed Group to raise money for us and left me out of the equation, he was behind the scenes doing something incredible. He was weaving his perfect story through this situation, and no matter what was going to happen or how many times I would go back to hospital, he was there, and nothing could change that. That conviction led me back to a place where I saw that Jesus was never late—not for Lazarus and not for me—because his promise is to never leave. So if his promise is that he never leaves or forsakes us, that means he has always been and he will always be there. Realizing these truths helped me to stop acting like a three-year-old throwing a fit and sulking in the corner and decide instead that I was going to face this trial head-on. This time I chose to face it, trusting God the whole way.

We live in a fallen, broken world, and I know that as I write this, someone somewhere is being born, and someone somewhere is dying. Someone is on one knee proposing and someone else is getting ready to file divorce papers. I know that as amazing things are happening all over the place, there are some very dark forces that are also at play. The Rob who woke up on Saturday, March 7, 1998, didn't have a hope in Jesus when he found out his brother had died. But the Rob who got a catheter inserted into his chest on January 1, 2014, did. I knew that how I chose to go through this trial would not only be an opportunity to show how awesome the God I serve is, but it would also be an opportunity to give hope to those watching my wife and me live through this. Our journey could possibly point people to hope in Jesus.

Jesus's promise in John 11 that Lazarus's sickness would not end in death came to pass even though Lazarus did die. See, our end is not Jesus's end. His promises are true no matter how dark it gets—and trust me, it got dark for Lazarus. I mean, he was shut up in a dark tomb, completely hopeless until Jesus arrived.

In John 12, we read about Jesus and Lazarus having dinner with his sisters. This time, though, Lazarus was a celebrity, and people were glorifying God because he got sick. Talk about the first reality superstar: he was a celebrity because he got sick and died. Jesus had used his hardship and turned his misfortune into fame and glory for God.

You may be a believer, and you know what I'm talking about in those moments when you struggle to see Jesus as you go through a difficult time. I want you to know that he is always there. If it is the one thing you take away from this chapter, then please get that. I shared the pizza story and the amazing high we reached by raising all that support in the same chapter I talked about some of my lowest lows. I did this to show that bad things often come unannounced. On the brightest, most beautiful days, you may receive the darkest news.

We have to know that God knows. He has never been caught unaware by the troubles we face. Hold on to the truth that he is there, and even as the storms and the winds are blowing, look to Jesus. If he is silent, it's only because he's asleep and there's nothing to worry about—the boat isn't about to capsize. Or maybe you are going through something and you don't believe in Jesus. You don't know of the hope I'm talking about in this chapter, and you desperately need to know about the peace that those who follow Jesus have. It's as simple as asking him to be the center of your life. Do it and watch the darkness depart. It cannot stand the power of his bright light.

6

A Church Called Covenant

The more a church is tapped into the gospel, the more
transformative power will be present
by the Holy Spirit in that church.

— Matt Chandler

I think we like to believe there are more good people in the world than there really are. If I walked the streets and asked people if they thought they were good, honest people, most of them would probably say yes, and, in addition, would also believe that most of humanity is too. The troublesome thing about that is we know that we are not as honest as we would like to be—meaning that most people probably aren't either.

The other day, my wife and I were sitting at a fast-food restaurant that offered water from the same dispenser where you get soda from. If you ask for water, the person at checkout will give you a cup with your meal, and you don't have to pay for it, it's free. If you want to drink soda, you are given a different cup and charged $2. It seems a straightforward method, but unfortunately, it relies too heavily on the honor system, and no one really monitors the soda machine as you pour your drink. You can easily walk up to the machine with a water cup and pour soda into it.

That day, Lisa and I watched, curious to find out how many people would actually pour water into their water cups or push the lemonade button instead. The results were not surprising to me, as person after person filled their water cup with lemonade, or just blatantly put soda in their water cup. I don't want to be judgmental but there was a girl who drove up in a $40,000 convertible who poured herself a cup of soda she didn't pay for! The act of dishonesty isn't because people can't afford the $2, but rather, it's the fact that their action isn't being monitored.

In the hour we were there, we watched eight out of every ten people be dishonest when they thought no one was watching. If that example doesn't let you know that humans are not as good as we like to think we are, then just go to YouTube and search any video with more than a million views and read the comments. The video could be about a dancing cat or a skateboard trick or a song cover, and the comments will inevitably be a collection of rude back-and-forth chatter about race, sex, and any derogatory thing under the sun. If we're being totally honest, though, we don't have to go to Chipotle or YouTube to find this type of depravity because we live with ourselves all day. We know that goodness doesn't come easily or naturally, which is why we celebrate it when we see it.

The Good Foreigners

I had been lying in hospital for a few days waiting for an appointment to be made with the surgeon who would insert the catheter I needed to start dialysis. The only problem was that the healthcare system in Zimbabwe is not the best, and so there was trouble locating the catheter that I needed. The delay meant that I was in hospital needing emergency dialysis, and there was not a single catheter in the city available for me. We were told that it would take almost four days (if we were lucky) to order one from South Africa. But this was an emergency situation; my health was deteriorating daily. Now I'm thankful that I'm married to a very strong-willed woman, who wasn't going to let her husband die because the hospital couldn't find a hemodialysis catheter. Lisa drove around the city, four months pregnant, going from hospital to hospital looking for the catheter I needed until she found it.

So we had one piece of the puzzle but came up against more difficulties as we were told we also had to find a cardiothoracic surgeon to do the procedure, as the hospital didn't know any that were around in Zimbabwe at that moment. How many cardiothoracic surgeons do you know off the top of your head? So we had a catheter but no surgeon, and even if we did find one, we had to come up with $2,000 in eight hours for me to have the surgery done in time. This was all too much for us to take in and process. But somehow my wife found the surgeon, and we were now left with the miracle of finding $2,000 in what was now three hours to organize the surgery.

Zimbabwe's healthcare system is a cash-upfront system, which means even if you have health insurance, in most cases, you have to be able to pay a certain amount of cash before receiving any sort of treatment. We had health insurance, but it didn't cover those procedures up front, so we needed the cash. The problem was that we were out of money, as we had paid for other things up front before this moment.

Our church, the Base Church in Harare, had been helping as much as they could and had asked us to reach out to them whenever we came across any difficulties. So we called one of the elders in the church and told him that we needed the money. We knew our church didn't have any free cash just lying around; many people in Zimbabwe have just enough to cover their own needs. We were amazed to hear as we spoke to the elder that there had been a person in our church who had told the church leaders that whatever financial need Lisa and I would have, the church should let that person know. So the elder passed on word of our need to raise $2,000 before eight o'clock that night, and the person (whom we still do not know) said he/she would pay the bill.

Where I come from, people don't just have $2,000 to give away on a moment's notice. God had obviously gone before us and had prepared a way. This donor also helped me move into a more expensive ward, because I wasn't being taken care of properly in the general wards because of the shortage of staff, and I was getting worse. I had never been this sick before, so I had not experienced how bad the healthcare system was in Zimbabwe. Seeing the lack of resources at this understaffed hospital—which was one of the good ones, I might add—was heart-breaking.

In the midst of all this uncertainty, the bill was paid, and I was to have a catheter fitted, and I was to start dialysis the following day. Even though we had miraculously achieved so much, I was now very nervous about how difficult it would be to find both the equipment and the doctors to help if I ever had less than twenty-four hours to live in the future. My wife had asked our family doctor what would have happened if we didn't find the money in time, and he had said, "If you don't have money, your husband will simply die."

I thought about how many people die in Zimbabwe every day from a lack of having someone to help pay for medical procedures, or not having enough money for dialysis, or any other type of treatment. We aren't the only people who have faced a medical crisis in Zimbabwe. This became an area of trusting God every week, as it cost $500 up front for dialysis. Even though we were given donations from people whenever we needed the money, it wasn't a sustainable way of going about things, and we needed something more permanent to happen for me to survive.

I remember walking into my nephrologist's office after I had been discharged to ask about a huge bill we had received from him. I couldn't understand why the bill was so large, as I had only seen him for a total of ten minutes. He looked at me after I had finished questioning the bill and told me that he was the only nephrologist in the country and that I couldn't be dialyzed without him. He bluntly stated, "If you want to live, you need me, so just pay the bill."

Knowing I didn't have that kind of money, I broke down and wept in his office. I pleaded for him to help us out by spacing out the payments for the bill, but he wouldn't budge. My life had become an impossible nightmare, and I just wanted to wake up from it.

Even though the situation we were in was very difficult, there had been one awesome thing that had started happening from the very first day I had been in hospital. Bob Myers, the lead pastor at Covenant Church in Doylestown, Pennsylvania, had contacted me almost daily. He called to find out how I was and prayed with his church as to how they could possibly help in the dark time we were going through. Bob and a team of college students had visited us in Zimbabwe earlier that year to serve at our conference, but I hadn't spoken to him since they had returned to the United States. If I am being honest, I wasn't sure where we stood in terms of a continued partnership with Dare2serve because of some miscommunications during that visit. To put it simply, I wasn't expecting Bob to be there calling me, and certainly not every day. His heart has shown me what I should strive for as a Christian leader, to rise above the personal issues in order to reach out to people in need.

What I didn't know at the time was that Bob was being led by God to do more than just pray for me, but to actually step out and see if there was a way that they could help me in my hopeless situation. Bob put up a photo I had posted on Facebook in his church one week, asking people to pray about how they may be able to help me. That morning, a man named George Verghis, whose father was a retired nephrologist, came up to Bob and told him that he may be able to help. He looked at Bob and said, "If Rob is to make it out of this, we need to get him out of Zimbabwe."

These words stuck with Bob the whole day, knowing that if they didn't do something, I may die. Lisa started e-mailing my blood test results to Dr. Verghis to try and figure out why I may have been sick in the first place since none of the doctors back home could tell me that. We e-mailed back and forth, and the church continued to pray about what God was asking them to do help me. Bob continued to talk about me and our situation in the following Sundays, and many more people came up and wanted to help with our situation.

It was after one such Sunday that a doctor in the church, Robert Mino, approached Bob and told him that the new president of Doylestown Hospital had just started attending the church. Dr. Mino told Bob that he would reach out to him and see if the hospital could help with my situation in any way. Jim Brexler, the president of the hospital, met with Dr. Mino, and they came to an agreement that changed my situation completely. Jim told the church that if they could get me to the United States, Doylestown Hospital would admit me, run every test they could to find out what was wrong with me, and try to help map out the next step to get me back to good health. They were going to do it all for no charge at all. Talk about a miracle.

More people stepped up in the days after that, like Tom Sullivan, who had received an e-mail from Bob and was prompted by the Holy Spirit to step in and use his business contacts in the medical industry to help me if I needed a transplant. Another family in the church, the Wissingers, had a mother-in-law suite in their house and offered to take us in and give us the use of a car when we got there. The pieces to orchestrate a rescue were all coming together. Bob, who leads a church of 1,200 people, was working overtime to find doctors who were willing to take me on. I wouldn't be able to travel to the United States without one. They also needed a commitment from a hospital that did transplants to agree to admitting me if I needed a transplant to live. All of this had to fall into place before I could board a plane in Harare, Zimbabwe.

We had found hope in a very hopeless situation, and God had used a church thousands of miles away to help us. As we patiently waited in Zimbabwe to find out if we had found the right hospital, Covenant put together a team of very unique and talented individuals to accomplish this goal. Our local church in Harare was also coming together alongside my wife and me. We had meals brought to our house by people from different churches, and we saw other local churches help to raise awareness of our needs through various means. I was overwhelmed by the love the community of believers showed my family and me in that moment. I couldn't help but feel humbled as I saw young people selling cakes at their schools to raise money for my treatments, and older people baking and selling crafts to help as well. God was bringing people together around a very dark situation, and he was turning it into a beautiful testimony of how his people, united, are stronger than any darkness we could ever face.

The day came when we got the call that Tom and the team had the green light they needed from a Catholic hospital in Camden, New Jersey, confirming that they had the doctor and the team to take me on. I was so happy to know that the light at the end of the tunnel was at least in sight. My wife and I celebrated that day with much joy and jubilation. The least likely heroes had stepped out in faith with me and had placed themselves between death and this disease.

The Unusual Suspects

It would be a lie to say that it was all roses and sunshine at this moment, though. Don't get me wrong, the people God had used to rescue us in this situation had blown me away, but I was struggling with the absence of those whom I had invested much of my life with. I was hurting from the fact that I hadn't heard from some of the leaders in my home church when I got sick, and the fact that my closest brothers in ministry had contacted me very little (if at all) during this time.

Coming close to death had shown me who was important in my life in a way that only a situation like that could reveal. As I was going through dialysis and having catheters placed in my body, my father hadn't even seen or called me. During the times I was most afraid, I had only my wife; my brother, Takunda, my brother-in-law Boyd; and a couple of other friends by my side. My mom had called me, desperately wanting to know if she had to get on a plane to be with me because we all know no matter how old you are, when things get rough, you just want your mother. We told her not to make the trip and get herself in debt over it as she lives in Canada and it's very expensive to fly to Zimbabwe. God knew all of this, though, and we had our "second mom" Carol there every day sitting with us and being just like a mother to Lisa and me.

If you have ever been through something so serious, you will know that as you go through those difficult circumstances, you hope for certain people to be there. When they are not, it gives you a wakeup call. If you've ever closed your eyes and thought about what people will say about you when you die, if you're anything like me, you've imagined your close friends standing there giving heart-wrenching testimonials of how amazing you were. My close-to-death experience brought to the forefront of my mind a passage of scripture that talks about what really matters when we are deciding whom to help and how to help them.

The story of the Good Samaritan became very close to my heart, as I saw what was happening in those crucial moments. This story, which is a reply to a simple question a lawyer had asked Jesus, became so real for me. "Who is your neighbor?" is the simple question that prompted Jesus to share the parable. What Covenant

Church had done in pursuing a very difficult avenue to rescue a relative stranger who was thousands of miles away was the answer Jesus gives in this story. Your neighbor is everyone, even if they're on the other side of the world.

The lawyer wanted to know if we are to love our neighbor, then who is that person? In his opinion, it was too vague to just say, "Love your neighbor." He wanted to know when he had loved enough people to check the box on his religious checklist. With this parable, Jesus was pointing out that you will never be done loving your neighbor if everyone is your neighbor.

What Covenant Church did in this situation is so against the grain of most cross-continental mission partnerships. They showed that I wasn't a project they were pinning up in the foyer of their church to make themselves look good, but rather, I was a real person whom they cared for. They were saying I am their neighbor no matter how far away I am geographically, and it didn't matter how I had gotten myself into the situation I was in. Much like the Samaritan, they helped me without thinking about what would happen later. This church did something as a sign of their faith in God and took a huge risk in helping my family. In case you're not sure what story I'm talking about, let's read the parable.

> And behold, a lawyer stood up to put him to the test, saying, "Teacher, what shall I do to inherit eternal life?" He said to him, "What is written in the Law? How do you read it?" And he answered, "You shall love the Lord your God with all your heart and with all your soul and with all your strength and with all your mind, and your neighbor as yourself." And he said to him, "You have answered correctly; do this, and you will live."

But he, desiring to justify himself, said to Jesus, "And who is my neighbor?" Jesus replied, "A man was going down from Jerusalem to Jericho, and he fell among robbers, who stripped him and beat him and departed, leaving him half dead. Now by chance a priest was going down that road, and when he saw him he passed by on the other side. So likewise a Levite, when he came to the place and saw him, passed by on the other side. But a Samaritan, as he journeyed, came to where he was, and when he saw him, he had compassion. He went to him and bound up his wounds, pouring on oil and wine. Then he set him on his own animal and brought him to an inn and took care of him. And the next day he took out two denarii and gave them to the innkeeper, saying, 'Take care of him, and whatever more you spend, I will repay you when I come back.' Which of these three, do you think, proved to be a neighbor to the man who fell among the robbers?" He said, "The one who showed him mercy." And Jesus said to him, "You go, and do likewise."

In those moments, it seemed we had experienced what it felt like to be robbed as we watched our bank account deplete to almost zero. I had known what it felt like to bleed and be on my last breath on the side of the road with no hope. Kidney failure had robbed me and left me in desperate need of help. I had seen some leaders in my church (the priests) walk right past me, not even stopping to ask if I was okay. I had seen some of my brothers in Dare2serve (the Levites) not even suggest lifting a finger to help me. I was lying there without much hope in my tank, and God sent the Samaritan to help me. The least likely people I expected in that moment. It was the old ladies at my church who took it upon themselves to help me, and it was friends I hadn't seen or heard from in months who visited me daily. It was the unusual suspects who were at my side.

I shared my frustrations with some people at the time, and as we were working it out, I realized that it's not people who move themselves to help others in times of need but, rather, God who does the prompting and the softening of hearts.

Maybe you're reading this and thinking, *Rob, that's a little harsh to put your friends and church leaders out there like that.* But this is me being honest. If I hadn't felt that was, I would not have confronted them, and they wouldn't know that they had hurt my feelings and let me down. As we go through hardships in life, we need to remember, even as Christians, that we are imperfect people. We make mistakes and bad judgment calls all the time, and we need to be humble enough to not continue making the same mistakes. I'm learning as a leader that when I have hurt someone or misled them, I have to show with my actions—not just my words but my actions—that I understand and am prepared to try to make it right. Truly repenting is not just lip service—it is a total change in direction.

Jesus ends the parable with a command to the lawyer and the people listening: "Go and do likewise." I remember these words tugging on my heart after reading this story, and I wondered how I could also go and love a neighbor hundreds of miles from me in a similar way that we had been loved. Before we left Zimbabwe, I saw a headline stating 1 million children were out of school because they didn't have $12 to pay for school fees. Prompted by this, we raised enough money in three days (on Facebook) for sixty children in a remote village to go back to school that week. My brother, Pastor Rupiya, and I drove hours to personally pay for the children to go back to school, and we have been paying their fees and taking care of some other basic needs since then.

I didn't know these children, just like some of the people who had helped me didn't know me. When I got to that small village, something hit me. If we hadn't raised that money and driven out there, those children would not be going back to school. Even though there were still 999, 940 children out of school in Zimbabwe, maybe I wasn't the only person that day who had heard God say, *Go and do likewise.*

Later that week, my wife and I boarded a plane to JFK, New York, en route to Doylestown, Pennsylvania, to find out what God was up to next. Covenant Church saw me in my desperate need and had compassion for me. They picked me up and put me on an "animal" and were willing to take me to the inn to get my wounds bound up. The people of Covenant Church were my good Samaritans.

I guess the thing we have to constantly guard our hearts against is the notion that if we can't help everyone, we shouldn't help anyone. It's a narrow-minded way of going about life and is an excuse we give ourselves to help us quiet the conviction we feel to do more. The only way we can actually push back the darkness that we face on this earth is if we all respond to helping the one person we can help. Our motto at Dare2serve is "Love one and serve one," which is supposed to encourage people to just start with one person. Maybe if we actually celebrated the stories we hear of people who have gone out of their way and interrupted the busyness of their lives to do something good for someone else, more people would step out.

I can't think of one person who helped to get us on that plane who didn't have to pause from their busy schedules to get us there. Some of the people who were on the care team are CEOs of big companies, or surgeons and pediatric oncologists who have very busy lives, but were willing to step out of their day-to-day schedules to take an extra step to help a stranger. As I sat there that first night in Doylestown Hospital, I remembered the many times I had used my business as an excuse to not go and help those in need around me. I thought of the occasions I had simply prayed for someone and not gone the extra mile to pray for guidance and wisdom as to how I could practically help them.

Maybe as you've read this, the same feelings come to mind of a similar situation before you at this very moment. I will leave you with the words that have not left me since then: *Go and do likewise.*

7

The God Who Never Left

*On the cross God left Jesus so that we would never ever
have to know
what it would be like to be forsaken by God.*

—Unknown

I remember when I first started spending time with churchfolk,
I looked through the Bible to see if my name was in there. I looked
and looked and didn't find it, which made me doubt a few things
the churchpeople were saying to me. I mean, if God knew who I
was before I was ever here on earth, then why wouldn't my name
be in his basic instructions manual? What added to my concerns
was the fact that my friends' names were in the Bible and mine
wasn't. I had a friend called Simon, I had a friend called Matthew,
I knew a girl called Esther, and the list goes on. Even Knowledge
and Wisdom had their names in there (those are real names in
Zimbabwe, by the way), but Rob was nowhere to be found. Years
later, thanks to Google, I finally looked it up again and got a hit
on my name! I quickly flipped through my Bible to the reference
in Malachi 3:8 and read this: "Will a mere mortal rob God? Yet
you rob me."

I immediately closed the book and didn't look up my name ever again!

The reason why I told you that story is that our identity matters so much to us. I was looking to find my name in the Bible as a way of assuring myself that this great God knew me personally. I know I can't be the only one who has needed to know that at some point. We don't just care about our spiritual identities; but who we are and what we've made of our lives also matters to us a lot. If you want to know how important our appearances are (something that's a big part of our identity), just look at how much money is spent on cosmetic surgery every year in the United States. An article online stated that $10.4 billion was spent on cosmetic surgery alone in 2012. That amount is more than the gross domestic product of Zimbabwe in the same year. It's actually more than the GDP of most small countries.

We live in a time where image and appearance matters, and it doesn't just matter in the Western world either. With the growth of the Internet and our increased access to information, I have even seen this materialism and these identity issues in rural parts of Zimbabwe. You can drive to a remote part of the country and see the local markets flooded with knockoff Gucci and Dolce and Gabbana clothing. Everyone wants to matter and look like they're "something" even if they're not. We fall into the trap that says what people think of you matters more than anything else. That is a lie. What matters most is not what people think of you or what they say about you, but rather, what God thinks of you and says about you.

After spending some time in the United States, I have met people who have their identity so wrapped up in what they do as a career, where they went to school, or even the political party they belong to. It's literally the first thing that comes out of their mouths as soon as you meet them. He or she may say, "Hi, I'm So-and-so, and I went to Penn State." Or "I'm the CEO of such and such." Almost as though that fact is what makes them who they are.

Stating something of status almost gives a person an appearance of confidence and affirms him or her to go after the things most valued. The problem is that this is a false confidence, and the things you consider worthwhile can be taken away in an instant. When I'm preaching about identity, I say that I shouldn't know who you vote for before I know who you worship (even if who you vote for is determined by who you worship). Even if you vote a certain way because you are Christian, I still shouldn't know the information in that order. When you don't know who you are, or when your confidence is in something as fickle as a job or a school or how you look, it will make it impossible for you to go through hardships in life. A foundation of such fleeting achievement is like building your house on the sand and not on the rock (Matt. 7:26). It won't stand when hard things come your way. We only get to be on a strong and unmoving foundation when we know who we are in Christ and we have our confidence in that fact.

Who Does God Say You Are?

If I was to start with all the verses that point to who the God of the Universe says you are, this chapter would be as long as the whole book. So I want to hone in on two passages of scripture. The first is Ephesians 1:4–6.

> Even as he chose us in him before the foundation of the world, that we should be holy and blameless before him. In love he predestined us for adoption as sons through Jesus Christ, according to the purpose of his will, to the praise of his glorious grace, with which he has blessed us in the Beloved.

This passage of scripture illustrates how intentional God is about His pursuit of us and also gives me confidence to know the extent of who I am to him, especially living in a world that is constantly trying to redefine that for me. He adopted me into his family and knew that he wanted it this way before I stepped into the scene. The word *adoption* is what settles it in my heart and shows me the gravity of how much a part of God's family I am.

I know a family that is in the process of adopting a child from Ethiopia, which, interestingly, a lot of the families in the church I am currently attending have done. This family is over the moon about the prospect of having another child in their home and are busy preparing for the arrival of their new addition. When their child arrives in the United States, his last name will already be changed and will be the same as theirs. This particular family already has their own biological children, so the thought crossed my mind about how they would treat their new member. As I watch the couple prepare their children for a new member of the family, they are making it clear that their adopted sibling will be as much a part of the family as they are. They will love each of the children the same, and will treat them equally and give them all the same benefits. There will be no difference between their adopted child and their biological ones.

Seeing this process put into practice changes how I look at the scripture about God adopting me into his family. He was looking at Jesus and saying, "We're getting Rob to join our family, and Rob is going to benefit from the same things that you benefit from." Jesus made the adoption possible by taking the punishment that I was meant to face, so that I would be a part of the family. If that doesn't give you confidence in who you are, then I don't know what will. If your boss at the big company you work for called you son, one day you would be over the moon even though we know that he doesn't mean you get the same benefits his children get. Now the God who created everything you see, the CEO of the universe, has chosen to call you son or daughter and give you the benefits that come along with it.

The second scripture I want us to look at is one that we've already looked at in this book. Isaiah 43:4 says,

> Because you are precious in my eyes,
> And honored, and I love you,
> I give men in exchange for you,
> peoples in exchange for your life.

Just to give context to that passage of scripture, God is talking to his people through the prophet Isaiah and is communicating his deep affection for them in this passage. The way I translate this verse to us today is that as soon as we're grafted or adopted into His family by accepting Jesus, we are God's people. Since God is the same yesterday, today, and forever, how he loves his children doesn't change from age to age. God loves you so much that he adopted you into his family and gave you a new name, his name (Isa. 43:7), and now he calls you sons and daughters (2 Cor. 6:18).

When I think of this, I am blown away by this reality. This is truly the gospel—the good news. That God would do this for you and I makes me confident in the midst of going through the hardships in life that we know will come. Being adopted into a family also means that we don't just take the good things that come with having that family name; we also take the hardships that come with being in that family. When people go into exile because they are being persecuted in their country, everyone else with that last name who stays behind and is related to the person faces persecution too. It's part of being in the family. Romans 8:16–17 reads,

> The Spirit himself bears witness with our spirit that we are children of God, and if children, then heirs— heirs of God and fellow heirs with Christ, provided we suffer with him in order that we may also be glorified with him.

This verse shows us that as we are identified as children, we are in a position to prepare ourselves to go through suffering with Christ as well. As we come to know God more, we start to see that there are many half truths taught out there that don't necessarily reflect the views of the Bible. A lot of the junk we have to war against is messages that talk of suffering solely being connected to our sin or a curse, yet the very Book we read is written by people who went through very difficult things for the sake of the gospel. Maybe if we identified both the blessings in our lives as well as the suffering we go through as signs of God at work in us, we would have more God-glorifying churches out there.

Where I'm from, pastors talk a lot about the blessing part of being adopted into the family and often leave out the part where you may have to suffer too. We call this kind of teaching the *prosperity gospel*, but in truth, there is nothing gospel about it at all: there is no good news in false advertising. Time and time again, I have seen people sucked into the lie of thinking that they can manipulate God with money. What kind of God would he be if he needed me to pay him to perform, or for safety and protection, like a mafia boss or a corrupt politician? You end up with people who attend these churches, giving their offerings with the wrong motives as the pastor gets richer and richer. And when the promised promotion or blessing or healing doesn't come, they walk away from God altogether. We will explore more of what the hope of the gospel is and the prosperity in the gospel in the next chapter.

God's Promise

After eight days of being in the hospital in a foreign land, being poked and prodded every day so the doctors could figure out what was actually wrong with me, I finally got the results from all the tests they had performed on me. The doctors came in and told me that I had what they called a pancake kidney and confirmed that I actually only had one kidney even though I had been born with two. They explained that the other kidney didn't develop after I was born, and it had disappeared as I got older. The US doctors told me that my high blood pressure misdiagnosis in Zimbabwe the previous May had caused my kidney to suffer more as the medication I was taking was damaging my one kidney.

There was nothing more the doctors could do for me to get my kidney functioning again, and they concluded that I would have to continue on dialysis until I found a kidney. I was in a foreign country, thousands of miles from home with no health insurance, and I was looking at needing a kidney transplant in one of the most expensive health-care countries in the world. Throughout this whole process, part of my heart had been hoping that I would only be in the United States for a few weeks, be given a new innovative drug to get my kidney working again, and would be back on a plane to Zimbabwe in no time. I wanted it to be a quickly resolved problem that would somehow sort itself out and be a story that I would one day tell my children as we sat around the dinner table. But it was quickly becoming apparent that it was not going to work out that way, and that I would be on this journey for some time to come.

My background in church didn't help me to process this reality. I was exposed to what I term *incomplete teaching* for some time before I became a real follower of Jesus. Before I go into this, I would like to say that the church I belonged to in my youth is doing some really amazing things in Zimbabwe, but when it came to the prosperity message part of the church, it was more an enemy of true discipleship than a friend. When I regularly attended the church, there was a big Nigerian prosperity movement that brought in misleading teaching. This movement taught about different levels of giving to the man of god "pastor" that would unlock different levels of monetary blessing; like there was a way we could barter with God. I think those teachings, when taken out of biblical context, could be very harmful to true discipleship and are not centered on who Jesus is but, rather, on what Jesus can do for you. This made the overarching theme of their message, if you are good then God will be good to you.

In moments during those first days of my diagnosis, where I found myself in a dark corner, my prosperity Christianity flared up, and I reverted to thinking that God's entire existence was to wait on me day and night. It may sound absurd or foreign to you if you have not been exposed to such teachings, but when you discover the freedom of actually being in Christ and knowing he is enough, you have to unlearn all the flaky teaching that you have learned. God led me to Isaiah 43 to really get this truth drilled into my heart. He was showing me that many pastors—especially in churches that preach the health, wealth, and prosperity message—will make promises that God did not make to his people. They may use scripture out of context and ask their congregations to base their entire spiritual lives on those passages. I was led to see that God does make promises to us, but those promises don't say that hardships will not come our way. God tells us we will have troubles and we should be prepared for them to come. Sometimes the very hardships that we dread are the very things that will propel us into our destiny. God's promise to his people in Isaiah 43:2 clearly shows that there are going to be some hardships to navigate.

> When you pass through the waters, I will be with you;
> and through the rivers, they shall not overwhelm you;
> when you walk through fire you shall not be burned,
> and the flame shall not consume you.

When is the key word in this passage of scripture, and it tells us that something is definitely going to happen. *If* is a totally different word, because the word *if* suggests that something might happen, but it's not definite. Had the scripture used the word *if* instead of *when*, it would justify the notion that we may not go through difficulties when we follow God's instructions. Jesus reinforced the truth of this idea by saying in John 16:33,

> "I have said these things to you, that in me you may have peace. In the world you will have tribulation. But take heart; I have overcome the world."

This statement was said as Jesus was telling his disciples that they were going to face hard times and would need to buckle up for a rough ride. By using *will*, Jesus guaranteed that there would be tribulation for his followers. When we revisit what I spoke about earlier concerning the hardships we dread catapulting us into a greater destiny, we don't have to look farther than Joseph's life in Genesis for an example. Joseph faced great persecution at every turn, being sold into slavery by his own family, being falsely accused of attempted rape when he was actually taking a stand for purity, and then being used by a fellow prisoner and left to rot in a cell.

At every moment Joseph took a stand for what God had placed within him or shown him, there was great difficulty. Yet if you read the story to the end, Joseph's difficulties were the pathway to the destiny God had for him. Yet Genesis 50:20,

> "As for you, you meant evil against me, but God meant it for good, to bring it about that many people should be kept alive, as they are today."

Joseph tells the very brothers who had sold him into slavery that what they intended for evil, God had used not only to help Joseph but also to save an entire nation from starvation. If we go back to John 11 and the death of Lazarus, we see the same scenario playing itself out. Lazarus got sick, and Jesus said he would not die. Then before you know it, Lazarus has been dead for four whole days. Jesus used the sickness and Lazarus's death to show just how powerful and mighty God is, and it served another purpose too—that of drawing the lost to him.

I have been experiencing this firsthand as Lisa and I walk this very hard road as a family. My brother has come to the faith and started to walk with God for the first time. Our story has been published on the front page of the *Philly Enquirer* local news section, and who knows how many people were able to read that? I can clearly see God using a difficult situation to draw people to him.

We can only see as far as the moment we're in, yet God can already see the whole picture and knows why we are on the path we're on and where it leads us to. The promise is not that we won't have to go through hardships but, rather, that God won't leave us to go through the hardships alone. "I will be with you" (Isa. 43:2) is the promise that I read in scriptures time and time again. He also promises us that the fire will not consume us even though we will be in the midst of it. As we go through hardships, we can have peace, and our thoughts can rest in the knowledge that God is with us rather than being consumed by our current situation. The second part of Isaiah 43:2 shows us a promise that three young men relied on years later in Babylon. They had to walk through the fire and hold on to God's word in that passage.

In Daniel 3, we read of a situation involving three very impressive young men who had found favor in Babylon. They were worshipping God and doing what they knew would please him; yet some haters, the Chaldeans, weren't having it (Dan. 3:12). The king was furious and ordered these young men to be thrown into a fire for not conforming to his request to worship something other than their God. They needed to be punished.

I can't help but think that these young men, as fearless as they were, were remembering what God had said about going through the fire and not being consumed. They didn't have to make the promise up—that's what the prophet Isaiah had been told to say years earlier. As these young men went into the fire (which the Bible says had been turned seven times hotter than usual), the king took a peek into the furnace to see how these young men were roasting, only to see not three but four people in the fire.

> Then King Nebuchadnezzar was astonished and rose
> up in haste. He declared to his counselors, "Did we not
> cast three men bound into the fire?" They answered

and said to the king, "True, O king." He answered
and said, "But I see four men unbound, walking in
the midst of the fire, and they are not hurt; and the
appearance of the fourth is like a son of the gods."
(Dan. 3:24–25)

He was amazed first of all by the fact that these guys were not
consumed by the fire, and then the fact that there was a divine
figure in the fire with them. Nebuchadnezzar didn't know it, but
as these young men were in the worst place they could possibly find
themselves, the person who joined them in that place was Jesus.
God had kept His promise of not leaving them in hardships, and
his promise that the fire would not consume them.

Facing Affliction with Joy

As this settled in and I started to look back at the last few
turbulent months of our lives, I started to find joy in the hardships.
Not happiness, but joy. These are often confused with each other.
I began to find joy in the fact that the thing I have wanted to do
with my life more than anything is to reach the lost and use my
story to bring restoration to the broken. I started to think of the
many people whom God had opened doors for me to reach, and
the truth had settled in my heart in a very real way. I found myself
saying and believing the fact that I was already victorious, and that
no matter what would happen to me, I had victory in Jesus. I was
reading the story I just shared with you and being led to say the
things Shadrach, Meshach, and Abednego had said to the king
after he threatened to kill them if they didn't worship his idol.

Shadrach, Meshach, and Abednego answered and said
to the king, "O Nebuchadnezzar, we have no need to
answer you in this matter. If this be so, our God whom
we serve is able to deliver us from the burning fiery
furnace, and he will deliver us out of your hand, O
king. But if not, be it known to you, O king, that we
will not serve your gods or worship the golden image
that you have set up. (Dan. 3:16–18)

As I was going through all the hardships and trials, I was conscious of the fact that God had never left me either. He was there when we needed the $2,000 in three hours to pay for my surgical procedure. He was there when we needed to be flown out of Zimbabwe to get to the United States. He had not left us even though the fire was burning around us. When we look carefully, we see that God is always there for us even when it doesn't seem like it. He never leaves. He never leaves, he *never* leaves. I was energized by the three men's confidence in God, whatever the outcome of the fire would be.

"Our God whom we serve is able to deliver us from the burning fiery furnace, and he will deliver us out of your hand, O king. But if not." I love that line—"But if not." If God doesn't deliver us, we still won't buckle under the pressure; we will continue to defy the king's request. I was finding that the threat of dying and not making it through this trial was no longer a threat for me but a welcome fight that I was now willing to face confidently with joy in my heart. It was around this time that I was told that we would need to raise $250,000—yes, a quarter of a million dollars—for the transplant process to go forward. It was huge news. I don't think I have used that much money in my whole existence. As daunting as that task would be, this time there was something different in my heart. I could see that even if I didn't make it through this, even if we weren't able to raise the money that was needed and I didn't get a transplant, I still got heaven! It was no longer a consolation in my heart, but now heaven was the ultimate prize that it was always meant to be. I was convinced that to live was truly Christ, but to die was also certainly gain.

When you read the rest of the chapter in Daniel, you will see that King Nebuchadnezzar was so amazed by what had happened in the fire that he became a worshipper of the Most High God (Dan. 3:28). Not only that, but he also made a decree that no one could speak against God (v. 29).

When we go through hardships, we must keep our eyes on the prize and our full trust in the fact that God is in control. In the book of James, we read that we should count it all joy when we go through trials of various kinds (James 1:2).

Before I understood what we were just reading about, I was convinced that James was using the word *joy* because English was his second language, and he used the wrong word. But now we know why we should count it as joy. James goes on to say that when we go through stuff, God is doing something in us that is ultimately leading us to a place of not lacking anything. Lacking in nothing does not mean having a Bentley or private jets but, rather, things of more importance than transient, material things. James clarifies what we may lack and what we need to ask for in verse 5:

> If any of you lacks wisdom, let him ask God, who gives generously to all without reproach, and it will be given him.

Our economy and what is of importance in God's economy are sometimes two very different things, which is why we should always look to his Word to guide us as to what is truly important. Romans 5:3–4 also puts into perspective going through trials and suffering for the sake of the gospel.

> Not only that, but we rejoice in our sufferings, knowing that suffering produces endurance, and endurance produces character, and character produces hope, and hope does not put us to shame, because God's love has been poured into our hearts through the Holy Spirit who has been given to us.

Paul is letting us see that when we go through suffering, we should rejoice, as God is at work in us. I know it can be difficult to get to a place where you can see difficulties and suffering as a source of joy, but I will say this, as I have said before in this book: any situation that requires faith is putting us in a position to please God. I love the way Paul ends the process of what God is doing in verse 4 when he says, "And hope does not put us to shame."

Hope is what we have in Jesus, and Jesus will not be put to shame. He is our hope, and he is the hope we hold on to in times of trouble.

8

Then There Was Hope

A baby is God's opinion that the world should go on.

—Carl Sandburg

On April 10, 2014, at 5:57 p.m., my life changed in the most dramatic of ways. Hope Paidamoyo Chifokoyo was born. In the midst of what had had been a season of madness, we received a miracle from heaven that day at Doylestown Hospital. I hadn't experienced love at first sight until the moment I laid eyes on that little beauty. I know about parental bias, but there is no parental bias here—she is one super cute girl. Lisa and I named her Hope because the word *hope* carries so much with it: so much promise for the future and so much peace and calm in turbulent times. (It also happens to be a word that is in almost every contemporary Christian song on the K-Love radio station, but that's not relevant.)

Above all those reasons, we named her Hope because we felt that God was telling us that we would never have to face another day without hope in our lives. It's a word that we now say 5,000 percent more often than we did before the tenth of April. As much as I say that now, we would not have to face another day without hope in our lives, the simple truth is that you don't have to have a daughter named Hope to have that reality. Hope is available to everyone and can be found in Jesus. In this chapter, I really want to explore the hope that we have in him.

Mountains into the Sea

We had been in the U.S. for a few months, and I had been going to dialysis treatments three times a week. We had just received the news that we needed $250,000 to go forward with the transplant option. At this point, there had been an outpouring of compassion from the community around us in Pennsylvania, prompting eighteen people to get tested to see if they were matches to donate a kidney.

Let's pause there.

Eighteen people, most of whom I didn't even know, had heard about what I was going through and were willing to part with one of their organs for me to live. It still blows my mind when I sit down and ponder how amazing the God we serve is. During that time, I walked into a meeting at the church and spoke to Bob and the missions pastor, Bruce Finn, about a fund that the church would be launching in the weeks to come. They told me that they were hoping to raise $100,000 in the first month to take to the hospital as a sign of good faith for my transplant operation before reaching out to other churches to raise the rest of the money. They were hopeful, but we all could sense that raising $100,000 in a month was a great big ask, and it would be nothing short of a miracle to achieve that.

I had been asked to preach on the launch weekend for the fund, and we were hoping to get a good response right away. At this point, God had opened numerous financial doors already with the dialysis center subsidizing a whopping $7,500 off my weekly dialysis treatments. In Zimbabwe, I had had one very arrogant nephrologist who wouldn't negotiate to give us a payment plan, but here in the U.S., I had been blessed with three nephrologists who had waived their fees to see me. We had already witnessed so any miracles, but I knew that we needed God to come through again. He had given us a good plan, which had been put together by some very godly, talented individuals. I went on to preach that Sunday and the church launched the fund that same weekend.

The week following the launch, I was sitting in the dialysis center watching something on my computer when Bob Myers called me. "Rob!" he said quite jovially as he always does. "Do you want to know how much money was collected during the services for your transplant?"

I immediately responded, "Yes!" I was not sure what he was going to say.

"We raised $67,400 in cash in addition to $122,600 in pledges with commitment dates for when those pledges will be fulfilled!"

I was blown away, and I know I say that a lot, but I really was! We had potentially raised $190,000 in one weekend when we were only expecting to do half that in a month. It reminded me of what the scripture in Mark 11:23 says:

> Truly, I say to you, whoever says to this mountain, 'Be taken up and thrown into the sea,' and does not doubt in his heart, but believes that what he says will come to pass, it will be done for him. (Mark 11:23)

It felt at that moment like we had seen a mountain go into the sea. Once again, in this journey, there was no denying that God was moving all the chess pieces at the right time to make everything come together perfectly. The church, which had already done over and beyond what most churches would do, had once again come together and made a mockery of any glory the enemy ever thought he might get out of this situation. We were well on the road to a story that would bless many people, and it looked like I might actually get to see the end of it as a healthy person. There are always two things I think about when it comes to money and the church. The first takes me to a place where I see people putting all their hope in money, and money becomes their savior rather than the God who provided the money. The second thing I think about is the abuse of money in church and the distortion of what Jesus did for us, and why He did it. We will look at these two separately in relation to going through hardships.

The Hope of the Gospel

As a result of getting this money, which by the end of the month had reached an astounding $237,000 just from Covenant Church members, I was put on an expedited transplant list. It basically meant that if someone who was a registered organ donor died and was a perfect match for me, I would get a call. Simply put, someone would have to die for me to live. Wow, let that sink in for a second. Someone who was living and breathing and going about their lives, maybe with a little daughter of their own, would have their time end on this earth so that I could live.

The crazy thing was that the concept wasn't so foreign to me because this had already happened. A young man had died at the age of thirty-three to give me, Robert Itayi Chifokoyo, life. The only difference is that this man died for everyone on the planet, and everyone who receives him as Lord and Savior will find life. His name is Jesus Christ, the hope for all men and women. Jesus is the hope that we were all seeking before we became Christians, and he is the hope all those who aren't following him are looking for. Jesus is also more than enough. He is more than all we need.

One of the hardest things for me to wrap my mind around was the question, why do we need Jesus? I mean, why couldn't I just be good all by myself and work my way into God's good books? We live in a time where we not only have identity issues, but, as Matt Chandler says in his sermon, "the Just Judge," "We love justice." I was listening to a sermon Matt Chandler preached about how Hollywood has grasped the fact that we love justice. This is why there is a *CSI* show for every city in America and a *Law and Order* episode for almost every crime committed under the sun.

"We all love justice until we are guilty," Chandler went on to say. How true is that? We really enjoy seeing those who break the law be brought to justice. But we too have done wrong. Which brings us to the truth: that if we serve a just God and we have sinned against him, therefore earning our wages (which the Bible says is death), then someone has to die for God to be just. God so loved us he put together a rescue plan like the one we read previously in Isaiah 43. God does the ultimate hostage negotiation and gave his Son in our place to pay the debt that we owed. By ourselves, we are not worthy to stand before a Holy God. We needed one who was spotless and without sin to take the punishment and clothe us in his righteousness, which is his rightness; therefore justifying us. There was no way around the obstacle without Jesus sacrificing himself for us, and then being raised back to life. We could not do this on our own. He became sin as we read in 2 Corinthians 5:21.

> For our sake he made him to be sin who knew no sin, so that in him we might become the righteousness of God.

We are only good enough to be in the presence of God because Jesus clothes us in his righteousness and not our own. This is why the self-righteous group of the day couldn't stand Jesus because they wanted to work to be in right standing with God and boast about their accomplishment. But we can't boast in the work that Jesus did because it was a free gift to us. You can't really boast about receiving a free gift. You also can't work for a free gift; it just doesn't make sense. I was telling my wife the other day that working for our salvation is like being given a Picasso painting and insisting on paying something for it. I don't have much money, so I know I couldn't even make a dent on the payment for a $106 million piece of art. Whatever I could contribute toward that painting would just be comical. How much more comical is it to think that we could possibly contribute toward the gift of Christ on the cross? We were bought with a high price, and that price was Jesus's blood.

I was watching the news the other day, and LeBron James, easily the best basketball player playing right now, was on the move again. He had won two championships with the Miami Heat and was looking for a new challenge, so he was traded back to the team he started off with—the Cleveland Cavaliers. The announcement of LeBron's return was on ESPN all day and was the biggest sports news of the day.

I also watch the English Premier League transfers closely, and players are traded for millions of dollars every year. Every time this happens, it always starts a debate about who the greatest sports player trade ever was. Was it Babe Ruth from the Sox to the Yankees? Or Cristiano Ronaldo from Manchester United to Real Madrid? Those were all good trades, but for us, the best trade of all is Jesus, who was traded for us and then flipped the switch, activated his buyout clause, and came back from the dead after purchasing us, only to get back on our team. That's my mind, working very hard to describe the great exchange in sporting terms, because it helps me to understand it, but you get the idea. It was an amazing swap that altered the destiny of potentially every person born after that moment.

The thought of being unclean and not able to cleanse myself and do things on my own is a lot closer to home since I started dialysis. If you don't already know it, dialysis is a process where your blood is put through a machine to help clean the impurities out. Your kidneys do that filtering job in your body 24/7, and when they stop working, you get sick because your body is no longer able to get rid of the junk it used to throw out. All that buildup of toxins makes you sick and left untreated will kill a person.

The dialysis machine isn't quite like Jesus in this example, because it's not freeing at all in the way that Jesus is; but it does take out the impurities that you can't. During the dialysis sessions, I don't have to do anything except sit with two tubes attached to my chest. These tubes draw out all the blood in my body, filter it, and put it back clean, in the space of four hours, three times a week. I need this to happen every other day in order for my body to stay functioning as close to normal as possible.

In this case, if a foreign agent did not purify my blood, I would not be able to live. If I was in denial that I needed the machine to live, I would have died. I may not have died the next day, but it would have happened gradually, and within a month or so, Rob would have been no more. I had to accept that no matter how I might have looked or felt, I was sick and I needed the machine to help me, or it would end badly for me. This idea is how we should look to Jesus. We have to acknowledge our need for Jesus even if it doesn't look like we need him. The times I've spoken to my friends and family who don't want to follow Jesus, they have always said, "That's not for me." It shows denial that they need him. They are like me on a dialysis day when I felt well enough and didn't think I needed the machine's help. I had to remind myself that I was sick and needed it to feel better.

Often Jesus refers to his mission here on earth as being for the sick or the unwell. You don't have to be a rocket scientist to know that millions of sick people die every year of undetected illnesses. They died, and in many cases didn't even know that there was something wrong with them. In that scenario, there are many people going through this life who are spiritually sick without knowing it, who need the revelation of Jesus. There are people who will die spiritually, like the many who die physically because they had no idea they were sick. They need Jesus—not what Jesus can give them but what he has already done for them. This is why the prosperity message is something that is so damaging to the message of the cross.

The Prosperity in the Gospel

Have you ever been in a relationship where you know that the other person is your friend only because of what you can give him or her? I mean the type of relationship where you know that the other person only talks to you when they need something from you. You won't see or hear from them until they want to use you for something. Imagine on top of that, that the person always quotes you out of context and holds you to promises that you didn't make to them. Cap that off with them tarnishing your name among the very people you are trying to reach and help, because people can't separate you and that person. That situation is the prosperity gospel to me.

Almost every church that preaches these messages has a leader who thinks he or she is one inch below God; and the people following these leaders, if they were being completely honest, have more reverence for the men than for God himself. This message is probably the fastest-growing movement because these churches are making promises that tickle ears. The only person prospering in that building is the guy in the shiny suit collecting all the cash at front of the church.

I have seen it all—from people selling phone refill cards that allow you to "get a prophetic message from the pastor," to people walking out of church in their boxer underwear because they were told not to leave church without sowing a seed to the man of

God, in this case the seed was the actual clothes off their backs. If you have never been around this type of teaching, it will sound ludicrous to you; yet for some, this is their experience of who Jesus is and how his followers behave. The problem with this is that the nature of these ministries is not consistent with the nature and character of God and, more often than not, is an opposite or partial reflection of his message.

In prosperity churches (which most of these pastors would not appreciate their churches being called), the central focus is often a man and not Jesus. There are churches that have grown up in my home city, where the congregants pray to God through the name of their leader. Talk about saying "Thanks for nothing, Jesus!" with your actions and words. In my eyes, it is basically a movement that takes us back to the garden of Eden, where the church leaders today want to be God just like the serpent did, and where the followers don't want God but, rather, his power and blessings, like Adam and Eve did. The notion of putting money on the altar at the front of the church whenever you hear something in the pastor's message that you want in your life is not clever on the followers' part; but it is sneakily smart on the pastor's part, as he has sold you something that you already have access to. Paying to get what can't be bought is highly offensive to God, especially if the thing is free in the first place. Acts 8:18–22 reads,

> Now when Simon saw that the Spirit was given through the laying on of the apostles' hands, he offered them money, saying, "Give me this power also, so that anyone on whom I lay my hands may receive the Holy Spirit." But Peter said to him, "May your silver perish with you, because you thought you could obtain the gift of God with money! You have neither part nor lot in this matter, for your heart is not right before God. Repent, therefore, of this wickedness of yours, and pray to the Lord that, if possible, the intent of your heart may be forgiven you.

Even though this statement is clearly in the Bible, we still see people trying to buy things from God much like Simon did. The apostles' warning to him about thinking he could buy things from

God was so severe that they weren't even sure he could be forgiven for it. But week in and week out, there are people putting price tags on grace and anointing. This message is so misleading, people who are holding Bibles and who seem genuine at first glance are preaching to the unsuspecting. They promise things that are of no eternal value as being the key to fullness of joy, and just like the serpent in the wilderness with Jesus, they use scripture to do it. A quote that has stuck with me since I heard it and which helps me stay grounded in the truth when my "prosperity" tendency flares up is this:

> When was the last time that any American, African, Asian ever said Jesus is all satisfying because you drove a B.M.W.? Never! They'll say - did Jesus give you that? Well I'll take Jesus. That's idolatry, that's not the gospel. That's elevating gifts above Giver. I'll tell you what makes Jesus look beautiful. It's when you smash your car and your little girl goes flying through the windshield and lands dead on the street, and you say through the deepest possible pain. God is enough, God is enough, He is good. He will take care of us, He will satisfy us, He will get us through this. He is our treasure, whom have I in heaven but you? And on earth there is nothing I desire but you. My flesh and my heart and my little girl may fail but you are the strength of my heart and my portion forever. That makes God look glorious. As God not as giver of cars or safety or health. Oh how I pray that America would be purged of the health, wealth and prosperity gospel and that the Christian church would be marked by suffering for Christ. God is most glorified in you when you are most satisfied in Him in the midst of loss, not prosperity." (John Piper, "How Is the Statement 'God Is Most Glorified in Us When We Are Most Satisfied in Him' True for Those Who Won't Be Saved?" www.desiringGod.org)

Every time I read that quote, I am hit with a renewed reality of how powerful and liberating the gospel is. When *prosperity* is placed before the word *gospel*, it is no longer the good news. It is no longer good when you hear that you have to give money to a man to receive what has already been made available to you. Because of my church experience and lack of knowledge, I was so caught up in this stuff; and before I had a real encounter with Jesus, my experience of Christianity was filled with moments of thinking how I could manipulate a loving God to actually move in to my life.

That approach to faith gave me a foundation that made it hard for me to understand why I had to go through hard things. But the hard times allowed me to grow me closer to him. The hardships were more for me to grow than they were about anything else, and my doing whatever I could to avoid them would mean not reaching the destination I was meant to reach. My pain can be felt for the many people like me who are flocking to places where the label on the door says "Jesus is King," but when you enter the place, you find a human king sitting on the throne.

The turning point that made me leave the church I was attending after I got back to Zimbabwe was a specific morning when I walked into the building, I felt a voice in my spirit say to me, *If this is my house, where is the evidence? The real kings and queens of this palace have their pictures on the walls. Why are people more thankful to the pastor than they are to me?* I heard that voice, and I knew my time of attending that church was over. When you have entire institutions claiming to be all about God but are actually centered on a person, there's your red flag!

The true and incredible prosperity in the gospel is that we get Jesus. And he is enough. We get to live our lives serving him and worshipping him. We serve a jealous God who is very real about his glory; all you have to do is read the Bible to see that. What an amazing privilege it is to be able to rest in the gospel and to be allowed to gaze upon his beauty for eternity.

We All Get it Wrong at Times

Even though I've spent quite a bit of time breaking down some of the reasons why the prosperity church is an enemy of the kingdom of God, I think at times we are all enemies of the kingdom. We may just do it differently and in other less offensive ways. And as a cautionary note, I do think that we can become so "anti-prosperity" that we become "anti-gospel." If all you ever talk about is suffering for Christ, you can miss God completely. There is a very real balance we need to find. I also believe God wants to heal and bless and do all of that good stuff on this side of eternity. But I know that even if he doesn't do that, he is still good and he has already done everything I could ever possibly need on the cross. I think of the high price God paid to rescue us, and I know he's not going to give up on any of us in a quick second. I think of Peter and how Jesus was so patient with him as he stumbled along the way to become the man Jesus had always known he was going to be. Luke 22:49–51 shows us an example of this:

> And when those who were around him saw what would follow, they said, "Lord, shall we strike with the sword?" And one of them struck the servant of the high priest and cut off his right ear. But Jesus said, "No more of this!" And he touched his ear and healed him.

We are like Peter sometimes, fervently doing things "in Jesus's name" that he hasn't asked us to do. I don't know how many times I have essentially cut off ears that Jesus has had to put back in place. I think of all these different church movements doing things that are against God's Word, and I think, *There's another ear Jesus has to put back on.*

We all get it wrong at times, and it's sometimes in the most crucial of situations. I feel like when I do something wrong, Jesus looks at God and the Holy Spirit and says, *Don't mind him, he's new here.* If we look at Peter's actions in the garden, we also find that Jesus had asked Peter to stay up and pray so that he wouldn't fall into temptation.

Peter not only got the game plan wrong in the garden by falling asleep, but he also totally denied ever having walked with Jesus a little bit later in the story. He messed up big time. Often, before we face difficulties, God prompts us to pray so that we won't do the wrong thing when the heat is on. When we spend time with God, we are able to hear from him, and it gives us the strength, courage, knowledge, and wisdom to survive the situation. It also gives us the confidence to face challenges like Jesus did after spending time with the father in the Garden of Gethsemane. Maybe we don't even notice that we haven't been spending time with God until we are in a situation that requires the wisdom and courage we can only find in him, and we fail badly.

Prayer is a thing that we give a thought to once in a while and sometimes don't see the importance in until we are hard-pressed to do so. Before I got sick, I didn't ever give my kidneys a second thought—that is, until the day I found out they had failed me. I went about my life for thirty years without ever waking up in the morning and saying, "Thank you, Lord, that my kidneys are functioning." I treated them like an insignificant part of my body, yet when they stopped working, everything stopped working, and I was dying.

When we stop praying, we stop noticing the impurities in our lives, and we are not releasing them from our system. In other words, praying every day is like your kidneys functioning properly. When you stop, everything stops working. The longer we stay away from spending time with God, the more the quality of our decisions start to show that we are not close to him. We end up going on yesterday's spiritual fumes and start to try and guess the game plays like a guy who has skipped practice for the last few weeks (another sports reference to help my understanding!).

Prayer is an important part of who we are as believers, as it is our constant connection to our Heavenly Father and our constant source of life. So as I end this chapter, I would like to end it with a simple prayer:

> Father God, we come to you today knowing that you are able and that your love is all we need to get through the difficulties that we face on this earth. Lord, we ask that those who are reading this would know this truth and find rest in you. I pray that you would heal those who are reading this and are sick. I pray firstly for those who are physically ill, that you, Lord Jesus, the Great Physician, would touch each and every one of them. I ask that if the healing doesn't come, it wouldn't discourage them, but that they would be satisfied in you always. I pray, secondly,

for those who are spiritually ill and are in need of experiencing your liberating love, grace, and mercy. I pray that through the words on the pages of this book, they may find elements of that. I ask, Lord, that you would redeem those who are going around saying things in your name that are contrary to your Word and your character.

I pray that none of them would leave this earth without repenting. And I humbly ask that you forgive me for the times when I have done exactly the same thing. We ask that you forgive us for constantly looking for a formula for your blessings that doesn't involve getting to know you or going through the plans you have laid out for us. We thank you for the hope we have in your Son. We thank you for the gift of your son Jesus and the saving sacrifice of his life on the cross in exchange for ours. We are forever grateful for that, and we will eternally give you praise, honor, glory, and majesty because of what you have done for us. We love you, and it is in your powerful and beautiful Son's name that we pray. Amen.

9

Victory

"When I say I win I don't mean this day I'm in
I mean that day
when the grey skies fade out then I'm winning 'cause
I reign with him.

—Trip Lee

There is a very weird relationship that America seems to have with the sports the rest of the world absolutely loves. Wherever you go around the globe, you will find millions of soccer fans (or as I would like to rightfully call them, football fans). The 2014 World Cup has just ended, and it wasn't that big of an event here in the United States. I know, I know, you will say it was big, but let's be honest, the enthusiasm here based on population size in comparison to other countries was still small. I realized just how small it was when the Sunday of the final game came. Some avid soccer fans in the church had played a little soccer match every Sunday afternoon since the World Cup had started, which showed the type of enthusiasm I can relate to. So it was a shock when I read on Facebook that this group was thinking about missing the broadcast of the final game in order to keep their afternoon game going. It made me chuckle that they all voted to record the finals, play soccer as usual, and then watch the game later!

If you are not from the United States, you may laugh now. I thought how ridiculous it was to actually go through with that plan because they claim to love the sport. It is like suggesting we play flag football in the park while the Super Bowl is on! Who does that? Especially if you claim to be passionate about the sport. How boring would it be to watch a World Cup final after you already know the result? Imagine waiting for more than two hours to see one goal go in that you knew was going in anyway. It's the reason I can't watch any sports event that I already know the score for—it's not as interesting for me because I don't have any uncertainty or worry. The tension and emotions are taken out of the game, and I'm left with a dry anticipation. On the other hand, it's a little different when you know the result and you know that the game was very exciting, you just don't know the details. In that scenario, you still want to watch it because you don't know how or when the action is going to happen.

This is where we land in God's great story. We know the end result; we just don't know how the in-between goes or when exactly it ends. Girls, the parallel to this would be watching a romantic comedy. You know the ending (because, let's be honest, they are all pretty much the same), but you really want to know the *how* and *when* of the story in between. My friend Josh preached about this very thing a few weeks ago as he spoke about already having victory and going through life knowing the result: God has won.

When you watch a recorded game that you already know the result to, even if your team goes down two goals, or three goals, you don't panic. You know you win at the end of the game. An even better way of looking at this is to imagine we are not watching but we are actually playing in a match that has been fixed—even in the moments of blood, sweat, and tears, we know we win. The other team may not know that, but we do; so even when we get bumped and bruised or injured, we know that victory is certain. The Bible actually tells us that we will get these bumps and bruises along the way, but we have to stay focused on the fact that we are victorious. First Corinthians 15:56–58 says:

The sting of death is sin, and the power of sin is the law. But thanks be to God, who gives us the victory through our Lord Jesus Christ.

Therefore, my beloved brothers, be steadfast, immovable, always abounding in the work of the Lord, knowing that in the Lord your labor is not in vain.

In Christ we can go through this life getting bumped and pushed from side to side, but it's not in vain because we have the victory. I love the line that says, "We do not labor in vain." At times the enemy throws doubt our way. Why keep going? What is this all for? I love the fact that we are on an epic journey, and that God has chosen us to be a part of his winning team. The enemy may bump us and bruise us and bring afflictions to break us down, but God uses them to draw us closer to him and make us more a part of this victory. So while we wait for the final whistle, don't wait kicking and screaming, but do it with great expectation and excitement to be with our Father in heaven.

Pressed but Not Crushed

There is a song often sung in church called, "Trading My Sorrows," and one of the sections in the song says,

> I'm pressed but not crushed,
> persecuted not abandoned, struck down but not destroyed,
> I'm blessed beyond the curse for His promise will endure,
> His joy is going to be my strength
> Though my sorrow will last for the night,
> His joy comes in the morning.

I'm always energized when I hear that song playing, and especially when that part is sung. We all have an option when we wake up each morning to trade our sorrows and our pain, and to take up this victory every day. This song draws its lyrics mainly from 1 Corinthians 4:8–10, which reads,

> We are afflicted in every way, but not crushed;
> perplexed, but not driven to despair; persecuted, but
> not forsaken; struck down, but not destroyed; always
> carrying in the body the death of Jesus, so that the life
> of Jesus may also be manifested in our bodies.

It can be incredibly difficult to go through hardships, but if we can keep our eyes fixed on Jesus and the victorious end we already have, then it can help us get through the trials. We may end up being afflicted in every way, but we're not crushed. Even when we are afflicted, we are victorious. Paul, the writer of this passage, is not speaking from an ignorant place of no suffering but from one of serious affliction. He gives a list of some of the things he has gone through for the sake of the gospel, and it makes my situation look like a walk in the park on a sunny day.

If you read 2 Corinthians 11:16–33, you start to see just how many troubles Paul had to endure for the sake of the gospel. Yet in the scripture we just read, we see him say that all the pressing will not lead to crushing, and even though we are persecuted, we are not forsaken. Whenever I feel like I can't bear to go through another dialysis session or another day of coming home and not being able to hold my daughter because of the cramping in my arms, I am reminded that all the displacement and troubles we face will be worth it someday. Nothing we go through on this side of eternity can compare to what God has in store for those who love him.

When I stop and think of how much we have lost in the last six months, it can feel pretty heartbreaking. We had to move out of the house we were going to have our first baby in. We had a little nursery for her, and it was our space, a home that she could call her own. We lost our community and moved to a foreign land, to a very different culture where at times we felt alone and misunderstood. We could no longer meet our close family for coffee and have the chance to be real about how we were feeling with the people who know and love us best, or have dinner with our church friends whenever we wanted to. We felt purposeless. We couldn't serve the children we had grown to love and the community we called home. On top of that, the kidney disease itself can be very crippling, and at times I felt like a prisoner chained to a machine, hanging on for dear life. I had to drink very little amounts of fluid, or my heart could get overworked and stop beating. I couldn't shower or swim, and if there was any chance of rain, I had to cancel any outdoor plans. My skin was constantly dry because of the dialysis, which caused huge black patches to appear on my face that hurt when removed. I got cramps all over my body for hours on end, and I could barely move for twelve hours after my dialysis treatments.

To top it all off, I had to sit in a chair for four hours, three times a week, just to keep breathing. But the worst of all these things was the fact that I couldn't do the things most dads do with their daughters. At times, I couldn't even pick Hope up because of the pain in my arms and my back after the treatments. My heart constantly broke for my wife, who I know has so much in her heart to do and achieve. Lisa has put every dream in her life on hold to be by my side. I remember going to her graduation for her bachelor's degree and hearing all her professors tell me that if she didn't do her masters in social work, it would be a great shame. She had graduated top of her class and had been given the Social Work award in her final year. She accomplished all that just to sit beside a sick person halfway across the planet in a place without our community or any kind of tangible purpose.

We had plans: plans to preach the gospel, feed the hungry, clothe the naked, educate the poor, enlighten the wealthy, and have our little daughter grow up in a blissful home. We had plans, but we don't serve a God who plays by our rules or follows our plans. We can always trust, though, that his plans are perfect. We know that our daughter may be sleeping in a kitchen now, but that's not the story forever. And even if it were, it was not our will but his will. We rest in the truth that if that plan was God's plan, it would still be way better than our own. We need to be in a place where we are submitted to his will and are active members of his team.

Not Everyone with an Arsenal Shirt Plays for Arsenal

As I sit here typing this book out in a Starbucks coffee shop, I think of how much following God's will makes me a part of what he is doing. A few years ago, I had a thought that had never left me. I was in my room back in Zimbabwe watching a televangelist totally rip the gospel to shreds. It was the all-too-typical "Jesus wants you to be rich, and these are the three ways to get there" message. I watched for about ten minutes, and I was so annoyed that I turned off the television and went to bed.

That Christmas I had received an Arsenal Football Club shirt from my brother, and it was laid out on my bed. I saw it when I walked into my room and picked it up. The thought came to my mind: *Not everyone with an Arsenal shirt plays for Arsenal.* (Amazingly enough, this very week as I was having dinner at a friend's house, someone happened to mention that Arsenal was playing the New York Red Bulls in New Jersey the following Saturday. It just so happened that the man we were having dinner with had worked on building the Red Bulls stadium and could get me tickets! That's a dream come true for me. I got to watch the football team I have followed since I was a little boy—live!)

As it was leading up to the game I thought, *I will be in the stadium with an Arsenal shirt on, cheering with the rest of the fans. It will be amazing, and I'm going to enjoy it, but thankfully for Arsenal's sake, I will not be playing.* They won't be relying on me for victory. I mean, I could show up in my full sports kit with my football boots on, and they still wouldn't let me play. On the day, there would only be twenty players who can affect the game in any real way. Arsene Wenger, the Arsenal coach, has no idea who I am even though I have an Arsenal shirt with my name and number on it. I can carry it into the stadium, and no matter how bad things get out on the field, the coach will never call on me.

It's the same with us when we are unwilling to follow what God actually wants us to do with our lives. Remember, we spoke in previous chapters about how God's purpose is for our good, and that no matter how hard things get in life, it is for our joy at the end of the day. There are so many people wearing "Christian" shirts who have no desire to be on the field and do what our Master asks us to do. They go off on their own tangent and misrepresent the team.

God wants us to be involved in what he is doing. It is an awesome privilege to be allowed to be part of his amazing story of redemption and restoration. After living a life that you thought was for the kingdom of God, I think the worst thing to hear would be Jesus saying, "Depart from me for I never knew you." It's not always intentional when we fall out of God's will for our lives. Sometimes the things we go through wear us down, Satan gets a foothold and starts to run rampant in our spiritual lives. We are left with a shirt, but we are no longer on the team (or following God with our lives).

This is not just on an individual level; entire churches can fall into this trap too. When I first got sick and went into hospital in Zimbabwe, the specialist physician that came in to do the rounds told me something that can be related to our spiritual lives. I asked him why I got sick all of a sudden, and how it could happen to someone who was healthy the previous week. He replied, "Rob, you were well, but do not fool yourself. You were not healthy." He went on to tell me that we gauge health according to the appearance of symptoms, but most of the time, when people are very sick, the symptoms only appear when it is almost too late. Unfortunately, cancer is an example of this that we have all seen. Some people have a tumor that's been growing in them for a while before they start to feel unwell; and when they get tested, they find out how sick they really are.

We shouldn't be striving to just be well but, rather, to be healthy believers and healthy churches. We should be willing to assess ourselves honestly, with the Word and in prayer, and come to a place where we can truly follow Christ in all that we do. If we have to wait for symptoms to appear for us to realize that we're not healthy, it may end up being too late. At times I get so frustrated with myself when I feel like I'm not doing what God wants me to do, or that I'm just another one of those people who are trying to be "friends with benefits" with Jesus. I don't want to expect all the benefits of a relationship with God without committing or being willing to go through any difficulties that may come.

Who Is Welcome, Then?

So if Jesus might someday say to people who did all the things mentioned in Matthew 23:22, "Depart from me for I never knew you," then who gets in? God put it in a simple-enough way for me to relate it to others a few months ago. I had been asked the very same question by someone. An old song I used to listen to as a teenager came to mind: "As Long as You Love Me" by the Backstreet Boys. The lyrics in the chorus go as follows:

> I don't care who you are,
> where you're from,
> don't care what you did,
> as long as you love me.

I felt that even though this pop song was composed and written with a girl in mind, the lyrics are exactly what God would say to someone sitting on the sidelines, not sure if they can be part of his family.

God Doesn't Care Who You Are

Many people, myself included, battle with the fact that we feel we may be lacking something it takes to be a child of God, and that lack disqualifies us from being used by God. I read a really popular quote the other day, which said, "God doesn't call the qualified, He qualifies the called."

We walk around looking at our past, and maybe we have faced rejection in our lives that has affirmed those negative feelings, but we have to remember that God looks at things differently. In 1 Samuel 16, God sent Samuel to anoint a new King. He told him which family the new king would be from but didn't tell him any more specifics as to who he would be. Looking at Eliab, the oldest son, Samuel was sure God was going to pick him because of his size and stature, yet the answer from above was "No." This prompted God to say in 1 Samuel 16:7,

> But the Lord said to Samuel, "Do not look on his appearance or on the height of his stature, because I have rejected him. For the Lord sees not as man sees: man looks on the outward appearance, but the Lord looks on the heart."

God was showing Samuel that the way he chooses the ones he will use is not the same way that we go about it. You may feel like you are nothing in everyone's eyes, yet God may pick you instead of the more educated and better-put-together people around you. At the end of this passage, we find that God anointed the boy who had been left out in the fields to watch over the sheep (v. 12). God picked out David as the next king when no one had even thought to consider him. So we can stop walking around using our insecurities as an excuse.

Some of my fellow partners starting out in ministry need to hear this. Yes, you may be the no-name brand that nobody wants to touch or invest in, but if God has assigned something to you, be faithful. You will find purpose and fulfillment in it. Even if thousands of people never know you or what you do. I face this very same thing as I write this book. Who am I to do this, and why would God use me to write this story when I don't have the credentials for it? I'm still doing it, and I don't care what man says. I look to obey God and follow him despite how I feel.

God Doesn't Care Where You're From

We also carry this identity issue with us and use the facts of our origin as a reason why God can't use us. To keep pounding the same story home until we get it, I will use another sports reference. I was watching an ESPN special on Tom Brady, the NFL star quarterback for the New England Patriots. Tom Brady is most certainly one of the greatest "misses" in the history of the NFL draft. His game stats are phenomenal, and when he retires from professional football, he will certainly be a Hall of Famer. The thing is, Tom Brady was the last quarterback picked in the 2000 NFL draft. He was number 199. That is like being that kid who gets picked last during your PE class. Fast-forward fourteen years, and he is by far the most successful pick of that year. Out of all the 198 people who were picked before him, he has probably been the most successful.

In the Bible, Gideon would have considered himself the last pick, yet he was God's number one pick for leading the army. He was full of excuses as to why God couldn't use him. But if we look at his "draft class," we see that God used him mightily, far more than anyone else. If we read the story in Judges 6, we see that as the Lord was speaking to Gideon, he started by addressing him as a "mighty man of valor" (Judges 6:12). A man who was from the weakest clan in his area and who said he was the weakest in his family. Gideon thought he was the weakest of the weak, and yet God still wanted to use him to defeat their great enemy?

When I read this, I think of all the excuses that we make when the Holy Spirit confronts us. We are so busy coming up with reasons why not to obey, even when the Spirit is leading us into an amazing destiny. We have to keep drumming into our hearts and heads that God is not looking for the perfectly finished product. He gets the glory when he uses the unsuspecting no-name person and he is still using the underdog to do mighty things today. You are reading a book, written by a high school dropout. God is still doing things like that—using the weakest of the weak to show that he is great and mighty. The list in the Bible of how God used people from bad places or tough backgrounds is endless. The ultimate example of this truth is the family he chose the Messiah to be born into. God chose to use a young couple from a little town called Nazareth with no significance at all, to raise, serve, and protect the hope of the world. Nazareth was just a little town with no economy to speak of and a very small population. God still chose that community and entrusted them with this great purpose. He didn't choose the already-established and successful family, but he established the ones he chose. He used a humble carpenter's family in a humble town. It doesn't matter where you're from or what kind of background you have. The truth is God can and will use anyone as long as they are willing.

God Doesn't Care What You Did

We may also feel like we've done some things that totally disqualify us from being used by God. There have been countless times when young men and women have come to me and said that they have messed up so much that God could never use them. If you believe that God doesn't use people who have a less-than-perfect past, then you don't have to go farther than the first few books of the Bible to realize how wrong you are. God used Moses, a murderer who fled because he didn't want to face the consequences of his crime, to lead God's people out of slavery. God used David, a murdering adulterer, to write many of the Psalms and to be a powerful king in the lineage of Christ. And God used Paul (formerly known as Saul of Tarsus), a persecutor of God's followers, to write three-quarters of the New Testament. Paul himself wrote the following scripture to dismiss the lie that we reinforce when we say we've messed up too much in our past for God to use us. First Timothy 1:15 reads,

> The saying is trustworthy and deserving of full acceptance, that Christ Jesus came into the world to save sinners, of whom I am the foremost. But I received mercy for this reason, that in me, as the foremost, Jesus Christ might display his perfect patience as an example to those who were to believe in him for eternal life.

Paul was basically saying, "I am the worst of the worst, and I was saved as an example to all of you who say you may feel you can't receive this grace and be used by God." Paul was right too, because I don't know if anyone who is reading this has ever persecuted the church to the point of going from city to city to find Christians to arrest and put to death. The Bible even says when the first Christian martyr, Steven, was stoned, Paul stood there cheering the attackers on. He was the worst enemy of the church at the time, yet after meeting Jesus, he became one of the most influential people in the church. Even if you are worse than Paul or David, you still have the same grace extended to you. His grace is sufficient, and it is enough to cover every possible combination of things you may have done against him.

As Long as You Love Him

God is interested in you.

Let that sink in for a moment. He loves you more than anyone you know. How amazing is that? He doesn't care about who you are or where you're from, what you did or what you look like. He loves you and wants to have a relationship with you. He pursues us, and he gave up so much to be with us, and he doesn't take that lightly. "He takes pleasure in us," as the Bible says (Ps. 149:4) and takes great delight in us (Zeph. 3:17).

The entire story of Luke 15 is about God welcoming the lost home. In this parable of the prodigal son, the father ran to the returning son while he was still far off, and he embraced him and kissed him. As the son who had squandered all his inheritance on prostitutes and parties tried to explain himself, the father's response was to welcome him back with open arms, to bring out the best robe, to slap some bling on him, and have a party. I would encourage you to read that passage of scripture over and over again when you feel unworthy or when you feel like you've messed up too badly to run back into the arms of the father. As God's grace sinks into your heart and soul, it will free you to walk away from the condemnation the devil would have you feel, and it will draw you into the safe and loving arms of our Father in Heaven.

The Bible asks that we do two things, and after that, we're good to go. Jesus asks us, firstly, to love God with all our hearts, and secondly, to love our neighbor as we love ourselves. If we do these two things, we will see the beauty of knowing God. As we come close to the end of this book, I want to give every opportunity to you to reconsider some of the things you may have thought about how God sees you. I want to give you as many opportunities to come back to a place of knowing God as I can. To come back to a place where if you thought you knew him and found that you didn't, you could ask him to be Lord of your life.

This is the way we can experience victory in the midst of great affliction. No matter how big or small you think your affliction is, God wants us to be victorious in him, but also to have a clear understanding of where that victory lies. God desires that all men know him (2 Pet. 3:9), but he is also a perfect gentleman and will never force anyone to do so. The choice is always ours, but he will use as many ways as he can to show his love for you. I pray that the victory I have experienced may also be your victory, and the grace that has freed me may be the grace that frees you, and that someday I will meet people who I never knew on earth who will remind me of the words on these very pages being used to bring freedom in other people's lives.

10

A New Beginning

*Now is our chance to choose the right side. God is holding
back to give us that chance.
It won't last forever. We must take it or leave it.*

—C. S. Lewis

I remember as a child swimming and playing a game with my friends in the pool. We would say to each other, "Let's see who can hold their breath under water for the longest time," and then proceed to take one huge breath and go under the surface. The longer you could stop yourself from exhaling, the longer you could stay underwater, and potentially win the game. It wasn't necessarily breathing in again that brought relief but, rather, it was the freedom that came from exhaling the pent-up air that felt so good. When you exhale, it releases the pressure of being underwater and gives you what you need to endure a little longer underneath the surface.

Right now, I feel as though I'm going through life and waiting to exhale. It feels as though I have been underwater for a while and I'm in desperate need of letting some air out. The words on these pages have been a way of exhaling, allowing me to feel free enough to get up out of the water and take the next big gasp of air I need. If I look back at the things God has done in my life, I feel as though I have lived most of it underwater, with moments of coming up for air before going back down under.

At this very moment, I am still sick, but I wanted to write a book about victory before the healing had come, if it were to come at all. I have been told by the hospital to have my phone on me at all times, charged and ready to receive a call that could tell me it's time to get a transplant. I have to be honest, though: there is nothing sure about anything in our lives right now; it's all up in the air. But I know there is no greater place to have things: up in the air, in the dependable hands of our Lord. The reality is, I may not even be allowed to stay in the U.S. any longer and could have to fly back to Zimbabwe and start the transplant process over from scratch.

At times, I feel that I may not even make it past the next dialysis session with how tough some of my treatments have been in the last a few weeks. In the midst of all that uncertainty, how do I find the relief that comes with exhaling? How do I find peace in my heart when I have ceased being able to provide for my family? Or when I do not get to decide what I do each day? When almost all the freedom a thirty-year-old man should have is seemingly gone? The answer is, I have to hold on to the truths that brought me to the place I am in and the victories I have seen in the past and draw upon that knowledge to see me through. I have to end this book the way I started it—by looking back and finding out why I was drawn to this amazing God in the first place.

Looking Back over My Shoulder

Faith

I walked into a local grocery store the other day, which had automatic doors to let people in and out. The thing about those doors is that they don't have handles on them, so you can't push them open—you have to walk confidently toward them, and if you are approaching on the correct side of the door, it will open for you to walk through. At times I think of faith like walking through those doors. We just have to walk with confidence and faith toward the door God has for us to go through, and it will open.

Another thing I noticed about the doors is that they have an Entrance Only sign on one side and an Exit Only sign on the other. I almost walked into the wrong one because I wasn't paying attention. If I had, it wouldn't have opened. No matter how confidently you walk toward a door, if you are on the wrong side, it won't open at all. You can push and try and try again, but it won't budge until you pay attention, read the signs, and walk through the right side.

I feel as though God is constantly telling us to pay attention and stop striving to use our faith to open a door that we're not meant to go through. As I look back on my journey, I see how many times I have tried to walk through the wrong door. I have prayed and pushed and walked off shrugging my shoulders in disappointment and frustration instead of trying the other door right next to it. We need to continually look at the different signs and messages that God gives us: they will help us know whether we are trying to enter a door where it says Exit.

Faith is much like stepping through a series of doors to get us to where we need to go, but it is also something else. I know that faith is a muscle that needs to be exercised. Once we start using it, it will grow and strengthen and be used to do more difficult things. Sometimes our faith grows without us even noticing it.

I use the example of being in the U.S. as changing my faith from a medium size to a large. Every time I come to this country, I find myself going up a size in my faith. During worship, as I raise my hands, I know the people sitting in the row behind me are hoping I don't go even more charismatic and bow down before the Lord, because I always grow a shirt size due to all the fast food I eat and all my shirts that used to fit are now too small. To say the least, I reveal a little too much in that reverent moment.

We can grow and not even notice the growth until it is very obvious. I look back at my life and the faith that was required to move back to Zimbabwe in 2007. It was not the same faith that was required when I quit my job in 2012. And it is an even stronger faith that I need to have now. This faith was exercised and growing in me during those seasons to bring my family and I to a place where we can totally trust in God to get us through the trials we're facing. As we step out in faith in different areas of our lives and we see God come through for us, we are given boldness for the next step, which may be even tougher.

Obey

The more we obey God, the more we can see that our obedience is leading us to a place of greater joy. We start to see that no matter how difficult things can get, God is always drawing us to obey him so that we can find more life rather than less. Looking back, I see the importance of obeying God's voice in even the smallest of things. I remember the coffee table where Bud and I sat months ago in Harare. That first meeting, seemingly insignificant as it was at the time, turned out to be one of the most important meetings I have ever attended. Meeting with Bud that day saved my life years later. If you had asked me then if that was the most important meeting I had had that month, I probably would have said it wasn't. But today, it is the only thing I really remember doing then. I may have done countless other things that I believed to be significant during that time, but it was this meeting that would turn out to be the most significant. I don't even want to think about where I would be if we both hadn't made the time to meet that day. It was a seemingly small thing to obey, but it is almost immeasurable how significantly it changed my life. If Bud and I didn't meet up, I wouldn't have met Bob Myers later on, and I certainly wouldn't be in Doylestown, Pennsylvania, today.

So many other amazing things have stemmed from that meeting, which shows me just how much we underestimate the power of listening and responding to God's prompting, especially when it seems insignificant. My encouragement is that we can continually draw on these small things. I can't tell you how many times I've put together a seemingly insignificant video for someone, or shared a message at a small gathering, or stopped to have a simple conversation, only to have it be used to get connected with someone else or see God use that "small thing" greatly in my life. Be where God wants you to be, and go where he asks you to go; it's for your good, trust me, I know.

Facing Shame

There is a passage of scripture that says that we are a new creation in Christ Jesus (2 Cor. 5:17), and reading that verse should free us from all the junk in our past. Don't get me wrong, one of the hardest things I wrote down in this book is my failure in the area of sexual purity. I don't know what people will do with that information, and if they will be able to move past that area of my life to hear my heart. But I was confronted by the Holy Spirit, and I asked myself, *Is that how you look at people who tell you the same thing?*

Of course, I don't, but I still think that this is one area in which people quietly suffer because of the judgmental attitudes that always come up about this issue. If you are a new creation, it means you are just that: new! I am burdened for young men and women to find freedom in this area and to be able to confess their struggles to fellow brothers and sisters so that they don't have to be bound by this sin.

Coming forward and saying you're not perfect is not a bad thing. Everyone knows that we are not perfect people. We are not living in a make-believe world; we all know that we fall short of the mark daily and that we shouldn't judge others. The amount of pride it takes to walk around judging people for something that you fail at too is huge, and this arrogant posture doesn't draw people to freedom or to Jesus. The people doing the judging may well be in greater need of confessing sin in their lives than the people they are judging, but the truth is we all need to confess our sins. When we deal with our moral issues in the light, it extinguishes any power that the enemy is yielding from the darkness. When we expose sin, we are actually trusting God more; and every time we trust God, he does something amazing even if he doesn't do it immediately. I promise you this, he doesn't want us to walk around with shame hanging over our heads.

Water into Wine

In John 2:1–11, we read about Jesus performing his first miracle at a wedding in Cana. Let's read it to see what Jesus was communicating about the reason he came to earth:

On the third day there was a wedding at Cana in Galilee, and the mother of Jesus was there. Jesus also was invited to the wedding with his disciples. When the wine ran out, the mother of Jesus said to him, "They have no wine." And Jesus said to her, "Woman, what does this have to do with me? My hour has not yet come." His mother said to the servants, "Do whatever he tells you."

Now there were six stone water jars there for the Jewish rites of purification, each holding twenty or thirty gallons. Jesus said to the servants, "Fill the jars with water." And they filled them up to the brim. And he said to them, "Now draw some out and take it to the master of the feast." So they took it. When the master of the feast tasted the water now become wine, and did not know where it came from (though the servants who had drawn the water knew), the master of the feast called the bridegroom and said to him, "Everyone serves the good wine first, and when people have drunk freely, then the poor wine. But you have kept the good wine until now." This, the first of his signs, Jesus did at Cana in Galilee, and manifested his glory. And his disciples believed in him.

Jesus was at a wedding, and something potentially devastating happened: they ran out of wine. In today's world, it's a little bit difficult to understand the gravity of that situation, because if we run out of something at a celebration, we go to the store and get more of what we need. A couple of thousand years ago, however, this was not the case. They didn't have grocery stores open all day just down the road. So when Mary came to Jesus and asked him to do something about the situation, she knew that they needed a miracle. The cultural context of this wedding was in a *shame culture*, meaning the worst thing you could do was to bring shame upon your family's name. So when Mary says to Jesus, "They have no wine," the statement was loaded with much more than what we see on the page. It wasn't about running out of a beverage, it was about a family's honor.

In those times and in that particular culture, if you ran out of wine, you could actually be sued by the guests at the wedding.

It may sound crazy to think that someone you had invited to an event could sue you for running out of a drink or food. But that was potentially what was going to happen to this unsuspecting family in Cana who were running out of the precious wine. They were facing impending shame and a possible lawsuit, and the bride and groom didn't even know it. The way Jesus responded sets us up for what we are talking about in this chapter—shame and guilt, and how Jesus handles it. His response to Mary was, "Woman, what has this got to do with me? My hour has not yet come" (John 2:4).

Those words—"My hour has not yet come"—are important in this passage. Every time Jesus talks about his hour, he is referring to his death. So why would he say, "My hour has not yet come" when all that is needed is more wine at a wedding?

Jesus was answering the question behind the question: "What are you going to do about saving them from their guilt and shame?" His response shows that what he is really saying to his mother is, "Yes, I know you know I have come to save people from their guilt and shame, but it's not a temporary guilt and shame that I will save them from. Rather, I will die to save you from an eternal guilt and shame."

Jesus came to save us from the very shame that hangs over us. When the Bible says we are now new creations in Christ, it means that this transaction has cleared. You are no longer the person you used to be; rather, you are a completely new person in Christ. No more guilt, no more shame. He took it all upon himself. Even though some people may only know the old you, you have to hold on to the fact that you're a new creation. Jesus eventually saves the wedding party from shame in the story of Cana. If he can do that, then he can take care of some of the things we face here on earth. But ultimately, He has freed us from the greater shame and guilt, and that is amazing news in and of itself.

The Next Steps for Us

As I conclude this book, and as I have exhaled on these pages, I am burdened to share some of my heart with you. My heart is still to be used by God no matter what my geographic location is. My heart is to obey the things that God asks of my family and

I—and not to obey him begrudgingly but with joy. One of the ways I see doing this is by writing this book and letting a portion of the proceeds go to a fund that Covenant Church has started. This fund will not only help me pay the bills that are to follow, but it will also help other missionaries who find themselves in the critical situation we are in.

At this very moment, I know of a woman with an amazing story who is lying critically ill in a hospital bed in Zimbabwe, in desperate need of assistance. We can't help everyone, but we can certainly open our mouths and help get the word out to serve and reach the ones we know of. Lisa and I are also heading up an initiative to get children back into schools in Zimbabwe, through our ministry Dare2serve and other supporting local churches. We hope to be able to send thousands of children in the Buhera district back into local schools, and also to provide them with basic needs and projects to help them stay on their feet. Mapping a way forward for the future leaders of Zimbabwe is no easy task, but it can be accomplished.

When I close my eyes, I see children running around freely, well fed, well educated, and experiencing the love they deserve. I see a church that is not trying to separate itself from the brokenhearted and poor but, rather, is willing to engage and come up with solutions for them. I see my wife and I standing in the gap for those little ones. This was what I was in the process of doing when I got sick, and this is what is still stirring in my heart to be done. It was to preach the gospel to the perishing and to reach those who are in dire situations with the hope of Christ.

God had other plans and led me to another land to preach, to instruct, and to learn how to lean on him and him alone. One day I pray to see Hope City Zimbabwe as a reality, and to see a church body be built that wholly lives to accomplish the things Christ set out to do on this earth. I pray to be used by God to bring him glory in everything that I set out to do.

In closing, my story is just that—my story. It is more personal and meaningful for me because I have lived it. But after reading this book, if there is something I want you to walk away with, it is this: always keep your hope in Jesus. Never stray from that hope or put it in something else; it doesn't work.

Always trust God when he asks you to do something. This leads to greater joy. Remember, sometimes the very trial you are trying so hard to avoid is what will actually propel you into your God-given destiny.

Lastly, if you don't know Jesus, get to know him. Maybe you were raised in the church and you have gone through the motions your whole life without really understanding God's love for you. If you have never needed faith in any way, start listening to God's voice and to his leading. He will guide you through life. At times, it may be difficult, but it will be the most fulfilling journey you will ever take. No matter what afflictions may come your way, when you walk on this road with Jesus, you will always be victorious.

AFTERWORD

What happened next has become one of the most monumental occasions in my entire life. As I quieted down, the Holy Spirit whispered to me again, words still bleeding love with every syllable, "If your Mom, or your Dad, or your Sister, or Grandpa or Grandma were sick, would you donate your kidney to them?"

"Absolutely!" I answered enthusiastically. "You know darn well I would. I would be on that operating table telling the doctor to 'cut me now' if it meant my family member could live to see another day!" As you can tell, I was pretty darn adamant about my conviction.

"Isn't Rob your brother?"

...

...

Silence... Complete, utter silence. My world had just been flipped on it's head and thoroughly shaken until all its contents lay scattered on the floor. In that heaping mess I saw everything I thought I knew and realized I knew nothing! And with God, that is the best place to be.

Suddenly, violently, I understood the implication of those words. For the past three years of my life I had followed Jesus with as much passion as I could muster, always asking for more. Yet my nearly sole focus had revolved around a vertical relationship with my Abba Father in Heaven. While that is a great focus it left out the fact that the cross has two-dimensions, *vertical* and *horizontal*. Jesus did not die and rise to life simply to reunite lost sons and daughters with their Father in heaven, I realized. No, He robbed the grave and stomped on hell to also reunite lost sons and daughters with each other. Throughout the Bible familiar phrases such as "brothers and sisters in Christ" and "my dear son in the faith" are used to describe believers. Now I could see why with the intensity of a millions stars' light. When anyone chooses to follow Jesus with their life they receive a blood transfusion. The blood of the Son of God immediately begins to surge through their veins. No one is ever the same afterwards, that is why they are called "a new creation" in Christ. This sentiment had a shocking conclusion though. If true, this meant that Rob was as much my brother as any of my biological relatives. If I had said I would donate my kidney to my biological sister, how could I hold back from the man Jesus said is my brother?

And so there I kneeled. Crumpled under the weight of revelation the Holy Spirit had just unloaded on me. Stunned by the depths of the thoughts of God. In awe of what Jesus, this One that I called the Lover of my soul, had accomplished over 2000 years ago. And silence was my surrender.

As with any process in life, though a decision had been made in my heart, there was much work to be done before it was realized "in the flesh" so to speak. Talks with my family led me to a place where I knew I needed to speak with the transplant hospital to acquire more information. It was then that I called and offered myself as a kidney donor to Rob. It was also then, that I was informed twelve others had beaten me to the chase.

Internally, relief mingled with a feeling that this process was not yet over. On the one hand, I figured, surely God was only testing me. Perhaps this was like the time God told Abraham to sacrifice his son Isaac but stayed his hand at the last moment. Perhaps this was just a test. But deep within the confines of my spirit, I knew that was not true. Often circumstances speak loudly, but the Holy Spirit was teaching me that His voice should always speak with more authority to us than our situations.

I gracefully thanked the transplant coordinator on the phone and hung up, thinking that maybe, it was the end of a test. A test in which I had learned a great lesson but nothing more than a test. But I knew better.

About a month later I received a call from the hospital saying they had reorganized the potential donor list. Though I had been number thirteen, I was now to be number three. The Coordinator assured me I would still not be needed but that she simply had to inform me of this change. But I knew that when God speaks, nothing any man says can stand up to or change His word.

Sure enough, one month later, I received yet another phone call. This time I was at work at the local YMCA, and though I heard my ring-tone, I was not able to pick up the call at that time. But I knew well who it was. I could sense it. When I returned the call, I was greeted by a polite but hesitant voice coming from the Transplant Coordinator. "Hi Michael, how are you doing today?"

"I'm doing well, thank you for asking. What can I do for you?"

"I wanted to call with an update."

"Yes, go ahead," I replied.

"Options one and two have dropped out of the donation process. I am wondering if you are still interested in moving forward with the process?"

Pause

This was it. I knew it had been coming but somehow things always hit us hardest when we come face to face. The silence did not last long but it was long enough for me to remember what God had told me. Long enough for me to remember what He had done for me. Long enough…

"I'm in." And then the roller coaster began.

In the next several months I saw every medical professional under the sun. Physicians, Social Workers, Nutritionists, Psychologists, you name one, I had seen them. I underwent test after test to ensure I was physically and psychologically ready for such a drastic surgery. At the end of it all, I was told that Rob and

I were a match, and pending an approval to extend Rob's medical visa, the surgery could be performed.

As the reality of the situation sank in, I realized that sooner or later I would have to tell Rob and Lisa that I was the one who would donate the kidney. Up until this point they had no idea that I was even pursuing such a course. Though we had prayed together and I had visited them during their time in the states, I had kept any information about the kidney donor process hidden from them. Partially I did this to protect myself from embarrassment if the process did not work out. Partially I did it to protect them from disappointment if I was not considered fit to donate. Whatever the reasons, it became readily apparent that now was the time they needed to know.

So, late one night, after a Bible Study hosted at my home, I accompanied Rob back to the home in which he and Lisa were staying. All I disclosed to him on the ride there was that I had something I needed to tell them. Rob, humble guy that he is, accepted this answer and we chatted away until we arrived at his place. He promptly gathered Lisa into the living room and when we were all seated, I quietly said,

"I don't know how to tell you this exactly, but I've been selected to be your kidney donor, Rob."

Silence. Then sobs. Tears of joy poured from all our faces as we allowed God to invade that moment. If ever there was a moment which could be considered "a heavenly moment," that was it. We cried and we hugged. We laughed. The "thank you's" were profuse and the love in the room was palpable. When the excitement simmered down and we had prayed I quietly exited their home with the conscious realization that the Lord had brought me this far, and what He begins in us, He is faithful to bring to completion.

Within weeks the final confirmation arrived: Rob's medical visa had been extended. This allowed the medical team assurance that he would be able to stay in the area to receive the necessary follow-up treatment for this life-changing surgery. With that matter settled a date was selected and locked in, August 26, 2014.

Any rational human being would suspect that I was scared in the time leading up to the surgery but I have to admit something quite odd. The feeling I remember before all else was peace. Total, utter peace. From time to time thoughts of fear would try to break in but never could they get past the wall of peace that Jesus had built up in my life. Day by day, I grew more convinced that this surgery was part of the destiny God had planned for me. To some this might sound like insanity. To me it was the very definition of faith.

With days to go before the surgery, Covenant Church rallied together in prayer. On the weekend before the surgery, Rob and Lisa, and I were given the privilege to share with the church all the "behind-the-scenes" work God had been doing. We were given the honor of blessing all those in the community who had given of their time and talent and treasure to make the surgery a possibility and now a reality. We were able to share all that the Lord had been speaking to our hearts in the past months and weeks. This was invaluable to me for the sole reason that I needed the world to know that my decision was predicated on a desire to embody Jesus' Love to the world. This was not a means for self-promotion or human gain. This needed to be all about God's glory or else not happen at all. That weekend settled matters in my heart and now I was ready for what came next.

And so I chose to walk to the operating table, where I would lay down my body, my life, as a living sacrifice to God. At any point, I was told, up until the moment I went to sleep under anesthesia, I could back out. The medical team would protect me and say they had found a medical problem preventing them from moving forward. No one would ever know why I backed-out. But I chose to walkthrough those gaping double doors, by myself, as Jesus did, and lay down on that table. "Here I am God. Send me. I'll go."

It was then that I realized how much Jesus Loves every human being on the face of this planet. While I was laying down for a surgery and would likely reawaken, He laid himself down knowing He would die, though He did not deserve to. The only thing that kept one foot in front of the other walking down that hall, for me, was the Love of God flowing through me. The only thing that kept Jesus walking up that hill, bloodied and bruised, was his love for you. My sacrifice communicated love and gave life to one man. Jesus' sacrifice communicated and demonstrated His love to all people, everywhere. My sacrifice pales in comparison to his, yet I am honored to have had the privilege to share in his walk even in such a small way.

In the end, I awoke from the surgery, complication free and grateful to the core of my being able to be alive. I was surrounded by a loving family and tons of friends as I recovered. Not a day went by without visitors and for that I am truly grateful. Rob's body immediately accepted the new kidney and he recovered even faster than I did. Joy beyond words filled my inmost being as I praised the God of Heaven for granting me the honor of having this story written over my life. See, it is not the story of a man saving another man, nor of a church raising enough money to save some random African guy. It is not a story that should begin or end with man. The true beauty of this story is that it originated with and ends with God. He Loved mankind and so He gave. He gave His own life. And because He gave, I can now give. And in that giving I have the honor of "re-presenting" His Love to the world. Perhaps the best part of all is that this story is not over because Love never dies. Just as I awakened from my surgical slumber, in an even greater way, Jesus rose from the dead to show the world that Love will always beat death. Love never fails. Love is alive. Love is always near to you. This chapter of my story has been written but your story is just beginning. My prayer is that you will choose to write your story with the ink of Love that flows straight from the Father's heart and into yours.

Many Blessings,
Grace and Peace,
Michael Wortell

Acknowledgements

When I started writing this book I had no idea what I was doing and to be honest I still really don't. I just know that for 11 days I went to a Starbucks and I bought a tall hazelnut latte and got to work. I have never read the acknowledgements in a book so I have to be careful that I don't forget the important people that helped me put this project together in one way or another.

I would like to first and foremost thank my Lord and savior Jesus Christ. Thank you for saving me from the pit of darkness I once thought was life. Your love for me blows me away and everything I do is for your glory and honor always.

Amy Harris for all your hard work editing my broken English, thank you!
To everyone at Xlibris publishing thank you for making this happen for me!
To my pastor Bob Myers for being a man who has poured so much into my life and for being bold enough to stand in the gap for me.
To my kid brother Michael, thank you for saying yes to Jesus. I'm living proof of your heart for our Lord and savior.
To my Covenant Church family and the amazing staff that serve them. This book is part of a story I could never tell without you. You are my family.

Steve Sargent for believing in me and seeing the potential in me even when I can't see it myself. South Ridge Church for helping me with this and for loving me and my family so well.

The Wissinger family, Bruce, Lu, Graham, Josie and Dawit I love you guys. Thank you for showing me what it really means to take in the foreigner. Lu thank you for the early morning rides to Starbucks.

Bud and Mands thank you for all your love and encouragement. I am ever so grateful for meeting you.

The "Rob care team" you are all dear and precious to me and the chapters in this book are a testimony of your faithfulness.

The medical team at Our Lady Of Lourdes and Dr Chakaravati, Thank you!

The Doctors and nurses at Doylestown Hospital and Jim Brexler, God used you guys to save me.

James and the Luke family for all your love, partnership and support. We are victorious!

The Base Church, thank you for your support and giving me an opportunity to serve God's Kingdom.

My mom for igniting a dream in me to someday write a book and for the innumerable sacrifices you have made for me. Love you momz!

The rest of my family all over the world thank you for supporting me guys, I love you!

Lastly I have to take a breathe and thank my beautiful wife Lisa. You have held my hand through every page of this book. Thank you for your encouragement when I didn't think I was qualified to write this and your patience when I didn't know how to. I am thankful for you everyday. Thank you Lis, for showing me what grace really means and what loving someone unconditionally looks like on this side of eternity. God has demonstrated how he lavishes his love on me by giving me the great honor of calling you wife. This is more than a book to you, this your story too. The tears are your tears and the joy is your joy. You are an amazing companion and an amazing mother to our daughter Hope. For that I am truly eternally grateful! I love you.

Victorious project,

We started Victorious to continue the work that Rob and his wife started in Zimbabwe, only this time we're involving a whole lot more people and you are invited. Our hope is to help build schools all over Africa but we have to start somewhere and thought that Zimbabwe would be a good place to do that.

Our aim is to help organizations that are building free schools in Zimbabwe, as well as help with the sustainability of their initiatives through the selling of our clothing. We have already raised $40 000 towards this and we are inviting you to join the many that have already given to this project. When you buy one of our products we will give a portion of our profits to build these schools.

To find out more please visit www.victoriousproject.com

Printed in the United States
By Bookmasters